An Instant in Paradise:

Collaborative Thoughts on Compassionate Empathy

Organized by Paul Jackson and written by the amazing WHWLSF team

ISBN: 978-1-7343551-0-9

Interior Design by MazeWaysLLC.co

Dedication

This book is dedicated to Jennifer and Samantha, whose contributions, insights, and encouragement inspired this project and everything I do; to my Mom who lives her life for others and who can create with brushes and color what I try to say in words; to my sister Therese and Aunt Trudy, who I admire so much and who can articulate so beautifully what I'm trying to figure out with *"the right words, in the right order"*, and to all the other anonymous and un-anonymous folks that contributed to this effort, including:

Dan Cerceo, Kimberly Gill, Michelle Jackson, Lolita Jardeleza, Gary Lafree, Betty Lafree, Ralph Mango, Sherry Mason, Michael Michlowski Jr., Mike Summers, and Fred Taylor (RIP).

All profits from this book go to Opportunities Inc. (www.opportities-inc.com/about)

INTRODUCTION

For those of you who read *"What Have We Learned So Far?"* – welcome back! For those who haven't, I hope you'll get a chance to read it.

"What Have We Learned So Far?" and *"An Instant In Paradise"* are efforts to come to insights through collaborative writing.

A note on the name of the book and title. The cover is representation of the statue of "Ali and Nino" (also known as "Statue of Love" in Batumi Georgia) and is based on the book, *"Ali and Nino: A Love Story"*, by Kurban Said, about star-crossed lovers trying to surmount the barriers of race, religion, and cultures. Once a day the two statues approach each other and for an instant become "one" while not actually physically touching. The title of the book combines this idea of momentary "oneness" and a quote by Abraham Maslow (the hierarchy guy) about self-actualization: *"We can get to heaven, but for five minutes. Then you have to come back to the world again."* After working on this project for the last year with my beloved collaborators, I have a view that the emotion of empathy might the closest we can get to what I think is the ultimate truth, which is union with others. And I think this empathy can be learned, taught, and cultivated. Another interesting thing about the

Nino and Ali book is that no one knows who wrote it – and lots of people have tried to find out who the alias "Kurban Said" is. Somewhat similarly, other than the last chapter, we have kept the submissions anonymous. I don't think this will generate the same about of interest in who "Kurban Said", but I think this approach has created a more open and intimate sharing experience.

In our first book, we shared out thoughts on the "big questions" – why we are here?, is there a purpose?, what happens after we die?

For this project, we tried to focus on how we relate and interact with each and our environment through the lens of empathy. This topic proved much more challenging, I think. It forced us to confront our limitations, our incredible capacity for cruelty, and indifference and to see what is left after this confrontation. But we persisted and hopefully you'll find it interesting...

Chapter 1: Let's Get Started!

Hi team, ready for round 1 of our follow-up to "*What Have We Learned So Far?*" I'd like to propose that we make our theme to be: "*Compassionate empathy,*" also known as empathic concern, which includes both understanding others and moves us to take action, to help, however we can.

I invite you to listen "*Just a Little Nicer*" Ted Radio Hour podcast (12/9/2016) and read the NYT article "*The Green New Deal Deal Rises Again*" by Tom Freedman (1/8/2019) and provide your thoughts on the very general topic of empathy – is it the emotion/skill/characteristic that we should collectively be cultivating?

Hagamos que suceda!

———

Responses:

The theme for this next project, moving on from knowing/learning to doing/acting, is interesting to me because I've struggled with it for some years. Clearly, the suffering of the world cries out for a compassionate response. Jesus couldn't have been clearer about tending to those in need; he also relates the story of the Good Samaritan. But HOW to help . . . there's the challenge. I don't feel temperamentally inclined to be a political activist although I give financial support and occasionally march. I chose a career in a helping profession and I realize that one-to-one relationships are much more to my liking than large group efforts. One belief that I have developed is that it is crucially important that one's action flow from true compassion and empathy rather than from ego-driven motives. If the action is driven by ego, more suffering will result. So, I think the activist has to do the inner work necessary and to understand the underlying motivations deeply enough to trust that love is the prime mover.

In previous contributions to this project, I've shared my image of each individual being like a small tile in a vast and astonishing mosaic. Every tile is necessary, whether it is monotone or brightly colored. Each of us must be who we were born to be, not what others or the culture expects us to be. I'm sure all of us can think of people who contributed enormously to the world because they were true to their own passions (e.g., Beethoven) and who were not social or political activists.

I interviewed a woman in her late seventies who is a retired history professor. She was educated in Catholic schools and raised in a

Catholic family. Throughout her adult life she has pondered the wonder and mystery of life. When asked about her thoughts on the meaning and purpose of life, she felt that those particular words didn't resonate with her experience or her way of thinking. "Purpose/meaning" seemed too objective or confident or clear in the sense of knowing reality. Rather, life seems filled with mystery and wonder. The more she reads and learns through conversations and experiences, the more her awareness expands and uncovers deeper mysteries.

The closest sense of deep commitment are to values of love, truth and understanding. Using those values as the gold standard, the northstar by which to navigate through life's decisions, they lead her through both the mystery and the ordinariness of each day. She does have faith in a Deity but acknowledges that there is far more that she doesn't know than what she does about God, creation, reasons for hope. She has a keen awareness that suffering and pain exist on our planet that is rapidly being despoiled. Despair and hope coexist but she has said "yes" to life and goodness. She wonders if perhaps God may be suffering and evolving along with creation and that, in a deep sense, all are connected and One. Despite her great appreciation of science and the scientific method, she readily acknowledges that her belief in God depends on faith. She believes that life is imbued with meaning and that it matters that she acts and lives based on the fundamental values of love, truth and understanding. But, as noted before, these beliefs and values are rooted in faith rather than scientific proof.

———

Several years' back, my friend Sherry lost her son, a policeman, at the age of thirty-five. At the funeral, a man, John, stood up and told the story that Sherry's son, fifteen years earlier, had questioned him about a burglary at a machine shop. The machine shop owner had identified John as the likely thief. Sherry's son told John that if he could locate and return the stolen tools, it would be the right thing to do. After the tools were returned to the owner, the owner still wanted to press charges against John. Instead, Sherry's son persuaded the owner to hire John, at minimum wage, mentor the boy, and help change his life.

At the time of the funeral in 2013, John was the owner of the machine shop. The owner had died a few years earlier and given the shop to him.

The funeral was the first time Sherry had heard this story. Since then, she has heard several similar stories of compassion by her son and by other police officers.

———

I was particularly interested in Robert Wright's thoughts on the "just a little nicer" podcast and the idea that empathy/compassion *"earned their way into the gene pool."* The notion that these traits were self-selected for survival makes a lot of sense and it also explains why empathy and compassion are usually reserved only for close relatives and close members of your inner circle.

Last weekend, I went to Evolution Weekend in Fulton Maryland. The topic of the discussion was the "Science of human origins." One of speakers, Dr. Briana Pobiner, with Smithsonian Institution's Human Origins Program, talked about the various species of humans who had lived and gone extinct with the exception of Homo sapiens. Two things in her talk struck me. The first one was *"The Old Man of Dmanisi,"* who lived about 1.77 million years ago. The Old Man of Dmanisi had no teeth and his jaw was severely deteriorated. Paleontologists believe that other members of his tribe must have taken care of him. Some believe this is the earliest known evidence of non-reciprocal compassion.

Another story that intrigued me was the story that, around 70 thousand years ago, the Homo sapien species may have been down to between 40 to 1,000 "breeding adults" and was incredibly close to extinction. At that time, there were at least two other human species – Homo Erectus and Neanderthals. Homo Erectus and the Neanderthals went extinct around 30 thousand years ago.

Within a relatively short period, the Homo sapien species re-bounded as the only surviving human species and Homo sapiens are now exceed 7 billion in population.

How did Homo sapiens survive this incredibly close call with ex-tinction? Did Homo sapiens evolve faster than other human spe-cies to develop the ability to empathize and show compassion for each other and realize their mutual dependence? Or, did they use their ability to work together as a collective to destroy the other human species?

I suspect that both were probably critical to the survival of Homo sapiens. After the lecture, my friend Rick said that he had heard somewhere that there is a close connection between humans' ten-dency toward violence toward "others" and our tendency towards empathy and compassion towards those similar to us. It's an in-teresting idea that these two traits might be closely linked.

I think we might be at a critical point in the history of our species – considering our population levels, the precarious state of our en-vironment, and the awesome powers of weaponry we have devel-oped – if we can't find a way to mitigate our evolutionarily-se-lected trait of identifying "others" and destroying them, Homo sa-piens, the last surviving human species, will probably follow the fate the other human species sooner rather than later.

———

Empathy is an interesting topic for me at the moment. I'd like to think that I practice compassionate empathy, but now I see that empathy comes in an unlimited number of shades and forms. Empathy is not a response to a cry for help or some other provocation, but rather, empathy begins with a pause. It's listening and understanding. Putting yourself in another's shoes. Trying to understand the feelings at play in someone else's situation. This all happens before a reaction or before offering advice or before expressing your opinion – at least it should be that way. Sometimes we feel like empathy is an obligation. If you are a decent human being, you should be empathetic, right? This puts us in an awkward position because we're walking a fine line that may lead us to actions that make us feel good – a selfish motivation. There's nothing necessarily wrong with that but it's not what empathy is about. Rather than, "It's not you, it's me," we should think in terms of "It's not about me, it's about you."

The basic premise of empathy is great but it's not quite fully baked until you take action. Action could simply be listening – really listening, or it can go much deeper.

Since this is my first attempt at writing in response to WHWDSF, I hope I'm not too far off mark. To summarize, empathy to me is a continuum of pause, listen, understand, reflection, and action. I was truly blown away by the demonstrations of empathy in my current situation. I believe that empathy needs to start with a common bond in order to thrive and really make a difference. One could argue that the fact that we are all human is the simplest way of understanding our connections and lead us to practicing empathy, but that bond is likely not strong enough. We need something more whether that is through shared faith, a community group or co-workers, or common circumstances; that bond that serves as a spark and a constant reminder that we are more alike than different and we really can make a difference in the lives of others even when we may not understand, agree with, or share exactly the same values.

———

Robert Wright's Ted talk about the evolutionary basis for empathy and compassion was really interesting. Our human brain is probably constrained by evolution in extending empathy to all. Even a hundred years ago, in an agricultural environment, if you helped everyone who needed help, you would most likely not survive the winter and almost certainly wouldn't be able to provide for your family and immediate circle. Empathy and compassion, from a human survival standpoint, could only be extended to a small circle of others.

There's a quote from Mother Teresa that I liked: "*If I look at the mass, I will never act. If I look at the one, I will.*" – I think she means that humans don't have the capacity to truly empathize with humanity as a whole and that all we really can do is show compassion to those immediately around us.

In today's society, however, I think this might be a problem. Especially in the U.S., our actions, particularly those who are in the top 1% affluent of the world's population, have an incredibly outsized influence on the outcomes of the rest of the 99% of the world when one considers consumption, the environment, trade, and political and military intervention, or non-intervention.

Somehow, I think we need to come up with a way to *"look at the mass(es)"* from a viewpoint of empathy in the decisions that we make (or don't make).

I hope this group has some good ideas on how to do it!

———

I liked the points that Sally Cohen and Krista Tippett made in the podcast: a couple of themes resonated with me:

- That empathy/compassion is something that should and can be taught or learned:

  o *"we have to find a way to relearn compassion"* (Sally Cohen)

  o *"we should treat becoming compassionate like learning to play a piano or throwing a ball"* (Krysta Tippet)

- The notion that humans are more emotional than logical and that *"what matters more is emotional correctness"* (Sally Cohen). Her point, I think, is that in the political and cultural debate about whether we as a society "owe" it to each other to help each other, no one is swayed by intellectual arguments – hearts and minds are changed through emotional connections.

———

In the last project, someone brought up the concept of the "Omega Point" – that we are headed toward a collective consciousness that doesn't distinguish between ourselves and others. Perhaps our current brain and cultural capacity for empathy and compassion that *"earned its way into the gene pool"* is the "seed" for us to go from "reciprocal altruism" to a true "compassionate" altruism.

I'm going to focus on learning more about this.

———

I liked Krysta Tippet's quote about: *"The terrifying and wonderous possibility of actually becoming one human race."* It seems like we are in an accelerating race between destruction and redemption.

———

I liked (and hope it's true) Karen Armstrong's view that compassion is at the core of all the world's great religions.

If that's true, and that we're are in a period of significant decline in religious participation, does this mean our collective level of compassion is or will decline?

It seems to me that perhaps we MIGHT be headed toward a more mature view of compassion – not demanded by an Old Testament god as the price to "heaven" but rather the way to live a happy, more meaningful life.

I also really liked her quote that if we can simply live the golden rule: "*All day and every day, you dethrone yourself from the center of your world, put another there and transcend yourself*" to the presence of god, nirvana, dao, etc.

Easy to say, a lifetime or lifetimes to do, but maybe the only thing truly worth our time.

———

I liked Karen Armstrong's comment that the world's religions emphasize that you cannot confine your compassion to your group.

Her quote from the Koran was good: "*We formed you into tribes and nations so that you may know one another.*"

———

I'm still trying to better define the very broad term: "Empathy." I liked the way Daniel Goldman broke it into the following categories:

- cognitive empathy - the ability to "read" other people's feelings
- emotional empathy - you feel what the other person feels
- empathic concern - "*I know how you feel and am predisposed to help you*" - this is the quality what we should try to develop to become a compassionate person.

I am really interested in learning more about what he described as "Social neuroscience," "new thinking that our default wiring is to help," his description of "mirror neurons" that allow our brain to "feel with" someone with whom we relate, and his comment that this default wiring is sabotaged by pre-occupation with self-absorption.

Fascinating!

———

I was laid off in 2018, I became immediately aware of the various levels of empathy in play and I truly appreciate them all. From those who took time to offer their condolences or simply ask how I was doing, to those that took immediate action and reached out asking how they could help – and then actually helped. I was overwhelmed by the response I received (without asking) and the continued support from family, friends, friends of friends, and what I would call mild acquaintances.

Although I had dozens of people reach out to see if I was ok, there is one individual that really stood out. I didn't have the opportunity to interview this person, but I think I can surmise what the answers might have been just short of truly understanding his motivation and actions of empathy. This individual, whom I would call a friend (but not close friend), has shown an uncommon level of empathy and concern for not only me but for others. First, he listened. Then he asked questions. Then he took action to help me network. He sent me job postings and has checked in with me regularly to see how I am feeling. I'm truly grateful for his empathetic effort, whether or not he realizes what he is doing. We are joined by a common bond in that we belong to the same parish and men's group — so I'd argue that for empathy to work, there needs to be a foundation in community. Values and some life experience are shared that allow for empathy in your interactions (he has been out of work, has a family to support, understands the challenges for people in our age bracket and overall situation.) What's really intrigued me was the persistence of the action. Checking in, following up, and continuation to take actions to help — what motivates this? Why continue after your initial empathic reaction, all without being overbearing? He doesn't owe me anything. There's no material benefit to him. I know this person well enough to make some educated guesses about motivation but what I really think drives it is the sense of obligation to our community; to lift each other up; to really consider everything at play – leaving judgment and options at the door – and carefully consider actions and their impact on everyone within the community. Can empathy surface without community? Perhaps but I don't think it's easy or natural.

———

Many years ago, I hit a bicycle rider with my car. I never even saw him, just experienced my windshield shattering in on me and a loud crashing sound. It turns out there was a witness who saw him make a left turn directly in front of me in the pouring rain. The man was unconscious during the entire time it took the ambulance to arrive and take him to the hospital. It wasn't until the next day I found out that he was alive and would recover. The incident put me into a fog of shock and dread that stuck with me for many months. One night, at a viewing for a family friend, of all places, I discussed the event with a relative. I think it was less anything she said and more the way she listened and the way she conveyed empathy after that the fog lifted. I hope I have the ability and opportunity to help someone out the way she helped me.

———

You challenged me to listen to a podcast, which I had never done before. After I learned how to find podcasts and some trial and error in finding the one you recommended, I found myself in an alternate universe where, per Sally Kohn, "Sean Hannity is Such A Nice Guy."

I ended up ordering her book *"The Opposite of Hate, A Field Guide to Repairing our Humanity."* This podcast also got me to order *"12 Steps to a Compassionate Life."* ☺

I thought the phrase: "*Being open to being surprised and changed*" went with your past questions about how to bring previous questions about how to keep from being isolated from people who disagree with you, i.e., listening only to Fox or MSNBC etc.

I have always kind of believed in what was called "reciprocal altruism." If you make feeding orphans a "good" thing, it makes it likely that your kids will be fed if you die. I also like the discussion about compassion being the root of religion and the discussion on religion can be manipulated to define identity and then used to feed war frenzy.

———

I liked the article by Thomas Friedman. I like how he explains why dealing with climate change needs to be more than a "*hobby!*"

- A couple other similar, should-be bipartisan ideas:
- Infrastructure: in addition to roads, bridges etc. maybe set a goal like a "bullet" train?

- criminal justice reform.

- making it easier for small business to get access to loans.

- prescription drug costs. I sort of view the drug companies as "Republican"

But I think some kind of plan for dealing with the burgeoning cost of older drugs could be "bipartisan," i.e., epi-pens used to be $16, now $321 and insulin used to be $12/vial, now $360/vial. Neupogen used to be $300, now $2100???

———

I liked Daniel Goldman's discussion on giving money to panhandlers. He said he gives money to almost anyone who asks for it. The bible passage: *"Give to everyone who asks you for something."* (Matthew 5:42) is pretty clear – it does not say to make a judgment on what the person will use it for.

I also liked the end of the podcast. Daniel Goldman's story of encountering a shirtless and unconscious man in a New York subway station that hundreds of commuters had stepped over to get to their train. Because his *"urban trance had been somehow weakened,"* he checked on the man and immediately, several others helped as well and the man, who had passed out due to hunger, was fed and revived.

It is a hopeful story.

Karen Armstrong's comments about the mystical powers of transcendence through the daily practice of empathy and compassion, as expressed by the golden rule of "Do one to others as you would want done to you," made me think of the "Man and Woman" sculpture in the seaside city of Batumi, Georgia. The sculpture is of two lovers, Ali and Nino, approaching each other in an embrace and, for a brief moment, once a day, merging into one.

Check in out on Youtube – search: "Ali and Nino Statue of Love".

———

In the podcast, one of the speakers said something like compassion is recognizing a person's right as a human. I like this definition because it applies to all humans, not just your family, friends, or people you know. You can feel compassion or empathy for strangers across the planet. We can feel empathetic for someone we hear about in the news in a horrible situation because they, like us, are human, and we can understand the sorts of emotions they may be going through.

Another speaker in the podcast said that empathy could just be a result of evolution, that over time, living creatures with the "biological molecules" that allowed them to feel compassion, were the ones that persisted. I struggle with this idea because I'm not sure who/what can feel empathy. The first speaker suggested it only applies to humans, yet the second speaker insinuated that animals (like our pets or primates) can also feel or be the subject of compassion. If compassion applies only to humans, I don't think our evolutionary past was long or rigorous enough to have permitted only the survival of the most compassionate people. Personally, I do not think compassion is a product of our biology alone, but rather something that is made possible because of our biology and is expanded through instruction and practice. I think a person who grows up without experiencing compassion will have a much harder time feeling or showing compassion.

I struggle with the separation between humans and animals. If you say that humans have the biological capacity for compassion but animals don't, OR both humans and animals have the capacity but only humans can truly learn compassion, then what about humans that lack those biological components or lack the ability to learn? Are we saying that people with mental or developmental disorders do not share in the humanistic realm of empathy? No one thinks that this would make someone less of a human but then what biologically sets humans apart from animals? Why are we the species that is special?

You might now be thinking that we are not, in fact, special at all. We're just animals with clothes. But I argue that there are a bunch of reasons why we are special. One of these reasons is that we are stewards of the Earth. No other species has the ability to control the fate of our world.

The article spoke about the Green New Deal, something that is supposed to inspire people to feel like they need to save our planet without inconveniencing themselves. I acknowledge that this is a smart idea due to the urgency of the situation and the disappointing politics surrounding climate change. However, practically every day, I am struck with the realization that humanity is killing the planet we call home, yet no one really seems to care. We are the most intelligent species on this planet, yet we are the species to destroy it. We are causing another mass extinction of the life we have the ability to protect. We are letting all other life down by not taking action. This is where I think compassion and empathy come into play. At some point, what we are doing to the rest of the Earth is going to become clearer to the average human. I think that compassion and our actions to save our planet will feed one another. As the environmental changes worsen, people

will start to see the horrible effects on wildlife and climate refugees, and that will grow compassion. As compassion grows, the
environmental effort will strengthen. As the environmental effort
strengthens, humans will grow more connected.

Climate change could be the thing that unites humanity through
compassion and I really hope people can start recognizing the urgency.

Round 2: Let's Dive Deeper

OK, based on your responses it seems like the topic of empathy might be worth some more consideration. This time, I ask you to listen to

- Listen to: "*How empathy works*" (Stuff You Should Know podcast 4/6/17) and provide thoughts and questions
- Want to dive a little deeper? Check out the New York Times piece on the topic of empathy: "*Year of Living Better: How to Be More Empathetic*" (Claire Cain Miller)
- Check out "*A mile in my shoes*" podcast

———

Responses:

"Imagine if we just had a way to increase our power production to meet our increasing demand AND reduce our carbon footprint at the same time?"

There's a new book out: "*A Bright Future: How Some Countries Have Solved Climate Change and the Rest Can Follow*" by Josh Goldstein and Staffan Qyist. It makes the case that the single most important thing we can do to reduce the impact of climate change is to make an immediate and massive investment in nuclear energy.

I haven't actually read the book but have listened to a terrific podcast with an interview with the author. In the podcast, they discuss the term *"virtue signaling,"* which is defined as *"the action or practice of publicly expressing opinions or sentiments intended to demonstrate one's good character or the moral correctness of one's position on a particular issue."* The author is critical of how companies, governments, and individuals "virtue signaling" about taking actions that do little to solve a problem.

The author also talks about the psychology of nuclear energy and describes the term "cross wiring" of our brains. It is when we are scared of one thing and then develop an irrational fear of something similar. For example, he believes the cold war and very legitimate fear of nuclear weapons transfers, in an irrational way, to nuclear energy. He also discusses how the weird coincidence nuclear accident in Three Mile Island happened at the same time the movie "The China Syndrome" was in the theatres that people conflated.

He also discusses how the MRIs used to be called Nuclear Magnetic Resonance Imaging but it scared people, so they just changed the name to Magnetic Resonance Imaging.

It reminds me how Kentucky Fried Chicken was concerned that customers were associating their brand with unhealthy food – so they changed their name to KFC.

Connecting this to this project's focus on empathy and empathy-based activism, I did some research to see if how the current "green new deal" deals with nuclear energy. In my opinion, this proposal focuses on renewables versus carbon reduction and therefore would result in a further reduction in the use of nuclear energy.

If it's true, and I think it is, that nuclear energy is the only interim solution to mitigating the terrible consequences of climate change, maybe the best thing we can do is to try to influence the current "green new deal" debate. Is anyone in this group interested in working on this?

Check out this podcast and let's get started? Check out: "*A Bright Future: How some countries have solved climate change*" (Give and Take podcast, episode 148).

———

Observations on Empathy as they relate to a reference made by Abraham Lincoln in his Second Inaugural Address, March 4, 1865. Source: Matthew 7:1-2 and Luke 6:37.

Matthew 7:1-2. *'Judge not, that you be not judged. ² For with the judgment, you pronounce you will be judged and the measure you give will be the measure you get. ³ Why do you see the speck that is in your brother's eye but do not notice the log that is in your own eye? ⁴ Or how can you say to your brother, 'Let me take the speck out of your eye,' when there is the log in your own eye? ⁵ You hypocrite, first take the log out of your own eye and then you will see clearly to take the speck out of your brother's eye.'* Luke 6:37 is basically the same.

The Oxford English Dictionary defines empathy as *'the ability to understand and share the feelings of another.'* Empathy should not be confused with sympathy. Sympathy is defined as *'feelings of pity and sorrow for someone else's misfortune'* (as in they had great sympathy for the flood victims).

These verses are among the most misinterpreted verses in the Bible. Jesus is saying that we should take a forgiving position and show mercy to others. In return, God will take the same attitude with us. We should treat others as we want others to treat us. This attitude of forgiveness does not mean ignoring or approving immoral behavior. It also does not mean that we should not try to help others. A spiritual work of mercy is to admonish the sinner. Many of us have used these verses as a way to shut down discussion of immoral behavior.

The real point of Jesus' message is to avoid being a hypocrite. Jesus warns us that our tendency to judge others is frequently based on our own personality flaws. This should be the prime thought before we judge others.

The passage asserts that we should always examine ourselves first to see if the splinter we see is actually affixed to our own eye and only if our eye is clean can we trust our judgment enough to begin the process of helping remove the offense from anyone else. This is an incredibly important point, both emphasizing the importance of good judgment and the steps necessary to acquire it.

If we cannot hold to the measure of how we judge ourselves, we have no right to applying that standard to others. I would argue the above was the intent of the Abraham Lincoln quote and what Jesus was teaching with respect to love of neighbor.

———

Fourteen years ago this month, I was hiking The Camino de Santiago in Spain. On the sixth day, I tripped, fell, banged my head on a rock, passed out and then fell (from the pictures) about twenty feet down a hill. On the positive side, I got my first helicopter ride. On the negative side and again, looking a photo of me in the hospital, I had black eyes, abrasions on the right side of my face and facial nerve damage on the right side of my face. My right pinky finger was broken, my left thumb was broken in three places and my right lung was punctured. All the doctors and nurses and everyone else were so nice. On the second day, I was moved to a room with 4 other women. After sharing stories, I decided my condition was the least serious. I was the only one in the room who could walk and always felt a bit better about myself when I could fetch things for one of them. Three days after my accident was the 2005 Madrid train bombing that killed almost

200 people. It kind of put things in perspective: in one part of Spain (Santiago), the medical staff are treating me and accident victims, while 600 kilometers away, in Madrid, the Doctors are deciding who to treat first, among the thousands of injured by the act of terrorists.

Some years later, I came across a quote by Ernst Hemingway:

"The world breaks everyone and afterward many are strong at the broken places."

I like that quote. I don't really believe in "lightning bolt" epiphanies but I do think that experience gave me a better perspective about my problems versus others. I think I am a more empathetic person now and, in some ways, I am stronger in my broken places. Although I still feel the spots where my bones were broken, maybe they are useful reminders to remember others in need.

———

I listened to the recommended podcast and gave the concept of empathy much thought. I am upset that the concept of empathy used in the podcast tied empathy to *"people who look like us"* and to tribalism. I agree that people tend to be more empathetic to people in their "tribe" but I disagree that people limit their empathy to "people who look like them," i.e., the same race and/or gender. I categorically reject that the default setting for human beings is racist and/or sexist. While I do not have a scientific study to link, I have watched young kids. Kids do not segregate or treat other kids differently according to race or, for the most part, gender. These traits tend to increase in some kids as they age. This shows that racism and sexism would appear to be a learned trait, probably learned from their parents or other adults. I would like to believe that humans are better with regard to racism and sexism than the implications of the podcast would imply. As I stated above, I agree that people tend to be more empathic towards people in their own "tribes," but I think that those tribes are very likely to have people of different genders in those tribe groups.

I also thought about how sometimes empathy is viewed as a weakness. People who are overly empathetic are made fun of or thought of as being soft or weak. I personally think that the world would be better if people were more empathetic and that more should be done to encourage empathy.

An interesting question, for me, would be to study how people's tribes' change as they move through various stages of life.

———

Yesterday, I spoke to a woman (yes, I am trying to try to strike up random conversations with people about empathy) and she told me the story about a family member years ago who was in an assisted care facility. The woman was starting to lose her cognitive skills; she couldn't remember things or people, would have conversations with people who were not there. Despite this, she was really focused on buying dinner for her caregivers at that facility. The old woman asked her to help her order the meal from her favorite Italian restaurant and knew exactly what appetizers, entrees, and desserts she wanted to order and for whom to order. The woman said that this experience (helping her elderly relative buy a meal for her caregivers) was one of the reasons that she started studying Buddhism and practicing meditation. She said, at the end of your life, when you are scared, in pain, or losing your cognitive skills, *"what will come bubbling out?"*

———

I have spent some time lately thinking about and reading about empathy. Since, as a group, we're heading toward advocacy, I think it's important to look at our motives to see if there's a hidden agenda. My hope is that when I advocate for a cause, the predominant motive is empathy (rather than, e.g., anger, desire for power or control, etc.) Some of the references given distinguish between sympathy (cognitive empathy) and emotional empathy. One comment was that *"empathy is from the heart; sympathy is from the brain."* The impression is that the former is warm and loving while the latter is cool and distant. I'd like to put in a good word for the cool, perhaps removed, position. The psychologist, Paul Bloom, points out that a patient wants his/her doctor to be knowledgeable and benevolent but not literally feeling the pain. A little "distance" helps the doctor be more objective. Someone who is continually focused on other people's feelings is in a state of "constant hyperarousal" which is unhelpful to everyone.

Surely, we do need to move from our tribal focus to compassionate action for all, especially those who seem most "other," and for mother earth. Justice and kindness and intelligence should be core values as I move beyond my comfort limits. Contributors have pointed out that either/or thinking blinds us from seeing that most actions have both positive and negative effects. The "intelligence" I just mentioned refers to a keen awareness of the complexity involved in trying to "help."

The recently deceased Mary Oliver wrote a very relevant poem.

AFTER READING LUCRETIUS I GO TO THE POND

The slippery green frog that went to his death
in the heron's pink throat was my small brother.
and the heron
with the white plumes
like a crown on his head
who is washing now his great sword-beak in the shining pond

is my tall brother.

My heart dresses in black and dances.

———

Might food conservation be a technique for developing empathy? My Grandmother lived for many years, well into her late nineties, in a retirement community. She got "Meals on Wheels" delivered to her Monday through Friday. She said that she was unable to eat all the food every day and it bothered her to throw food away (she lived through the Depression and both World Wars). She asked the Meals on Wheels people to deliver meals just Monday through Thursday and on Friday she made soup from the vegetables and other leftovers from the Monday through Thursday meals. She said she looked forward all week to Friday and the opportunity to make and enjoy a home cooked meal (and not have wasted any food). When I think of the amount of food our family throws away (leftovers find their way to the back part of the refrigerator blocked from view by new leftovers and ultimately turn into grotesque lab experiment-type transformations). That will be my focus: better planning meals, keeping the leftovers and perishables within sight, and eating the leftovers before making another meal. I think from my Grandmother's perspective, to waste food was disrespectful to the animal that was slaughtered, the farmers, and everyone who had helped bring the food to the table. Here's a website for me to get started: www.epa.gov/recycle/reducing-wasted-food-home.

———

Here's something that made me think of the general topic on empathy – a quote from the Buddha that there are two special types of people in this world – those who are generous and those who are grateful. The specific quote is the following:

> *These two people are hard to find in the world. Which two? The one who is first to do a kindness, and the one who is grateful and thankful for a kindness done."* — *AN 2.118*

I thought about this for a while. Do generosity and gratitude come from the same "place?" Are they more like synonyms (an emotion involved in a kindness to another) or more like opposites (giving versus taking)? Maybe if we could look at them as synonyms (we are here to help each other and sometimes we will in the role of being generous and other times we will be in the role of being grateful) we would be better at both giving and receiving.

Also, why are generous and grateful people special and *"hard to find in the world?"* I know lots of people who are generous and grateful. I am sometimes generous and grateful. I think, however that the Buddha is saying that we have the opportunity to experience generosity and gratitude at a much deeper and richer level than most of us currently do and that if we can do so, it is the path to the ultimate understanding; that we are interlinked with each other, with the creator, and with all of time and space in the universe to a degree we can't grasp. But if we can, we would experience a level of infinite connection and joy. I hope so.

This reminds me of a joke about the Dalai Lama ordering a hot dog – he asks for "*one with everything....*"

In trying to find the quote about generosity and gratitude, I ran across another Buddhist story that made an impression on my years ago:

"*Then the man, having gathered grass, twigs, branches, & leaves, having bound them together to make a raft, would cross over to safety on the far shore in dependence on the raft, making an effort with his hands & feet. Having crossed over to the far shore, he might think, 'How useful this raft has been to me! For it was in dependence on this raft that, making an effort with my hands & feet, I have crossed over to safety on the far shore. Why don't I, having hoisted it on my head or carrying it on my back, go wherever I like?' What do you think, monks? Would the man, in doing that, be doing what should be done with the raft?*"

"*No, lord.*"

"And what should the man do in order to be doing what should be done with the raft? There is the case where the man, having crossed over to the far shore, would think, 'How useful this raft has been to me! For it was in dependence on this raft that, making an effort with my hands & feet, I have crossed over to safety on the far shore. Why don't I, having dragged it on dry land or sinking it in the water, go wherever I like?' In doing this, he would be doing what should be done with the raft." — MN 22

In the context of empathy, the canoe might represent things we have accumulated that we are afraid or unwilling to give away or to give away with a generous spirit. As a result, we become burdened by our own possessions. Did you ever see the George Carlin skit on "Stuff?"

———

Just some quick notes on the "How Empathy Works" podcast:

- I liked the story (from Paul Bloom) about how babies are born with empathy and will comfort each other. Also, that characteristic similarly occurs among primates. (16th minute)

- "In group" and "Out group" behavior is something about which I want to learn more (19th minute)

- The "racial empathy gap" is sad – I'd like to learn more about this. Tribalism seems to be something that is evolutionarily built into us. How does tribalism relate (or not relate) to racism?

- Mirror neurons – this is really interesting topic

———

I was curious what the Koran says about empathy. Here's something I found:

> *"And what can make you know what is [breaking through] the difficult pass? It is the freeing of a slave, or feeding on a day of severe hunger, an orphan of near relationship, or a needy person in misery. And then being among those who believed and advised one another to patience and advised one another to compassion."*

I'd like to better understand what *"those who believed"* means in this context.

———

Interesting podcast. I found a lot of the concepts to be new information. The discussion about Sandy Hook was interesting. People sent thousands of stuffed animals to the town. It was a nice gesture that made them feel better but ultimately didn't really help anything at all. Then, despite unbelievable outpouring of anger/support/sadness, the gun legislation didn't change. My question for the group is this: I think the common notion when you interact with a charity is that giving money is good but it is better to get personally involved. That giving the gift of your time is very important. Do you agree and if so why?

This is topic I have chewed on a bit myself. I've spent a lot of time with the Haiti charity that I support. I have personally seen the value of my money creating long term change in the community that the charity supports. When I go to Haiti, I spend time doing work that one could pay Haitians to do. Given that, why not just give the money to pay the Haitians? I don't totally know the answer but I think it has to do with empathy and compassion. Because I have seen the value of my donations and others, I have formed a personal relationship with the people, and I care more. I also think that having seen it personally, I am better able to encourage others to donate. The other aspect of it is sort of reverse compassion maybe. I hope that the time I spend in Haiti builds a bridge to the Haitians. The children there can see that they are valued when strangers are willing to come and work/play side by side with them in their community. Maybe that will give them hope and pride in their community and in themselves.

——

I have wondered about the following: how many times, when talking to someone who suffered a car accident or fender bender, did they fault the other driver? How many times have you talked to someone who acknowledged that they were at fault? For me I would say its 100% vs 0%. Either I know only righteous, excellent drivers or most of us create our own stories about our lives.

Every day, on my way to work, I have to turn right (south) onto five lane road. It can take several minutes for there to be a gap in traffic to turn right. If the traffic slows down due to a backup, drivers will sometimes let you turn in front of them. I try to make eye contact with the driver in the right lane to appeal to them to let me in. When someone does, I have a feeling of connection with my fellow human beings. I always wave into the rear view mirror to thank them for their courtesy. When I let someone into my lane and they don't wave thank you, I feel a moment of annoyance – why can't they make a simple gesture of courtesy? A couple weeks ago, I had to go north on that road to run an errand, then found myself coming back and I was that driver in the right lane. I didn't find myself in the position of being able to slow down and let someone in front of me but I wondered whether I would 1) let someone in, 2) pretend I didn't see them, or (more likely) be completely oblivious to them.

Now that I think of it, driving in rush hour (hours) in the DMV offers rich opportunities to become a more empathic person.

———

The quote from the "How Empathy Works" podcast that struck me was: *"This is the challenge of our time – globalization by a tribal species"*

I think this quote is attributed to the primatologist Frans de Waal, it struck me as a powerful insight – our actions as humans are determined by our evolutionary path, which focuses on survival of the fittest, which includes some level of empathy as a survival characteristic, but also (I think) includes a characteristic for violence and destruction.

This probably has worked until now – cooperation and empathy within your family or clan – and unity in conflict with clans. But as the podcast articulates, we are at a crossroads of competing evolutionary characteristics – survival by recognizing our mutual self-dependency versus our evolutionary ego-focus on ourselves and our immediate family.

———

Our study of empathy - how important this activity is! Particularly as our country and the world beyond seem to become further and further divided. I was very interested in the different types of empathy. I have learned as I got older that I have a great capacity for empathy, in fact, that it can sometimes be (and probably has been) to my detriment. But I now recognize that type of empathy as affective empathy – experiencing another's emotion but without much action associated with it. But I've also learned through our podcast and reading that this is a great stepping stone to higher levels of empathy that can turn into action that (hopefully) can bring us together as a community.

According to Najmeh Keyhani, PhD Education & Curriculum Studies, University of Western Ontario (https://www.quora.com/What-is-the-difference-between-Cognitive-and-Affective-Empathy), there is a link between empathy and morality. The more evolved forms of empathy are associated with greater morality and morality brings people to action. She believes emotional/affective empathy to be the form that contains no morality, and cognitive empathy to have some. The most evolved form of empathy is adaptive/moral empathy, which goes beyond simply understanding others and sharing their feelings, has the highest level of morality and moves us to action to look for solutions and to create change.

When I think of empathy, I have always linked it with sympathy and viewed it as something that is used when someone is hurting, struggling, or otherwise dealing with 'bad times' or 'hard luck.' I'm coming to realize that it can and should be used for more than interacting with people that are dealing with sorrow or difficulties. Perhaps its best and most important use is for interacting with people that have different views from our own. We have become so polarized as a nation and interact with each with such vitriol — particularly through social media — we need to become more adept at 'walking in each other's shoes' in order to see other perspectives and learn ways to disagree without hate and violence and negativity.

My question related to empathy:

Technology, including online newspapers with the ability to comment on articles, Facebook, Twitter, YouTube, or anything that provides a public presence and voice, has brought us together in terms of the ability to communicate more readily with one another. Has this increased our ability to empathize with each other by exposing people of different backgrounds, cultures, and belief systems to one another? Or has the anonymity of the online community torn us further apart by making it easier to be less tolerant and more vocal about this intolerance when exposed to people that differ from us?

———

As we've been thinking about, researching, and discussing empathy over the last few months, the algorithms of the internet (Google and Facebook) have figured me out and led me to some thought-provoking content. I still think it's creepy that the algorithms can lead us to these bits of content but the existence of the content demonstrates that empathy is a hot topic – there is a need for understanding how to acquire and use empathy in our lives. Here are a few interesting bits that I've stumbled across that inspired some questions about empathy:

How do we practice empathy when we have so much to deal with ourselves?

https://www.inc.com/justin-bariso/there-are-actually-3-types-of-empathy-heres-how-they-differ-and-how-you-can-develop-them-all.html

An article on the impact of empathy in the workplace. Is empathy a skill that can be learned and developed?

https://medium.com/microsoft-design/empathy-for-organizational-transformation-f35768da9fa6

A touching story of empathy demonstrated by a chimpanzee. Is empathy an instinct?

https://www.facebook.com/watch/?v=634527357006406

And a quote from a blog I follow, Tiny Buddha. If we cannot solve problems for others, is empathy saying, "What's the least I can do?

Round Three: The Darker Side of Empathy

Here were the round three prompts:

1) To what degree are we responsible for the impacts of our empathetically-driven actions? For example, if you build a house in Haiti, are you depriving a Haitian laborer the opportunity to earn wages? Similarly, if you give a homeless person money and he uses it for drugs, are you financing a bad, illegal, and dangerous action?

2) Let's examine the darker side of empathy. Please read the following essay: https://www.theatlantic.com/science/archive/2015/09/the-violence-of-empathy/407155/

Or anything by Paul Bloom (who appears to be leader of the empathy "poo-pooer" camp) and provide thoughts on the negatives of empathy. What do you think: is more (and better) "what the world needs now?"

3) For those of us who are interested in the biological origins of empathy, who's interested in looking into this a bit more? Here's an article: A short history of empathy and a podcast: stuff you should know - mirror neurons

———

Responses:

To what degree are we responsible for the impacts of our empathetically (or non-empathetically) driven actions? I'm think I'm going to start with "*no*" at an individual level and "*yes*" at a more macro-level.

Let's start with an individual who asks for a dollar. I think that we are called to help this person. I say that because it feels like the right thing to do. On the other hand, we don't know if the person will use this money for negative purposes, to buy drugs or alcohol or, if giving the person money prevents him or her from getting the social services that they need. At this same time, however, I don't think it is our role to make judgments. Jesus said, "*Give to the one who asks you.*" (Matthew 5:42), not "*Give to the one who asks you, if they are going to use what you give them for the "right" purposes.*"

Similarly, I think the passage from Matthew 25:44-45: "*Lord, when did we see you hungry or thirsty or a stranger or needing clothes or sick or in prison, and did not help you? He will reply, 'Truly I tell you, whatever you did not do for one of the least of these, you did not do for me*" is pretty clear that Jesus is literally present in the people with whom we try to avoid eye contract when we pick up our step and walk past.

I'm not sure why this should be different but I do feel differently about the choices we make (or don't make) as a group, as a business, or as a society. I suspect that much of what we do in the name of good has unintended consequences of which I think we should make ourselves aware and reconsider our collective actions.

I thought the Paul Bloom article, "The case against empathy," was really interesting and a bit disillusioning. I started on this project with the view that more empathy is *what the world needs now* and now realize that it's not nearly as simple as that.

Paul Bloom's main point, as I understand it, is that the emotion of empathy comes from the same part of the brain where tribalism comes from - and everything that comes from tribalism - classism, racism, genocide. The empathetic notion of "feeling another person's pain" is reserved for people that look like us, people that "could be my own son." I listened to one podcast that mentioned the judge.

The article included a couple of questions to which that Paul Bloom didn't have good answers and I think these two questions are worth thinking about a bit more.

The interviewer asks the question: "*I've argued elsewhere that privilege has a way of blinding the privileged and that is a big reason why people fail to notice the role of luck in others. Obviously that political implications of this are terrible. I've always understood this to be an argument in defense of empa-thy"* to which Paul Bloom responded, *"I'm not entirely sure, but it's a great question."*

The second question is: *"I've always felt that identification with another's suffering was the key impetus for human solidarity and that empathy is a gateway to recognizing the commonality of experience. If we want to make the critical shift from solipsism to collective consciousness, don't we need something like empathy?"* To which Paul Bloom responds, *"I wouldn't say with confidence that's wrong."* An interesting comment by Paul Bloom is that: *"Empathy is a psychological process of imagination."*

So, overall, I'm still a fan of empathy, even if it's part of my reptile brain. I think that maybe the way to go is to actively cultivate empathy in ourselves and others with a clear understanding of empathy's limitations.

———

It's interesting that we are discussing this topic. There is a long-time running disagreement between my spouse and me. Every time I go to a grocery store, I grab a couple of carts from the parking lot, as many as I can, and roll them in. I feel "empathy" for the people, often kids, who have to go around the lot in the cold or heat rounding up carts. This annoys my spouse who says that over my lifetime, I will have eliminated one job for one grocery store person. Also, she doesn't like it when I pick-up recyclable trash when we are taking a walk?

But, by and large, I think people use possible misuse of charity as an excuse not to perform charity rather than for the benefit of the recipient.

Because I am a HUGE Darwinist, I believe there is a biological root to empathy. (war too!) If humans have empathy, they are more likely to take care of injured fellow humans instead of leaving them to die and to take care of orphans instead of leaving them to die. I also think this is the root of "tribalism." I remember that when I was a kid, I was told by a nun that Eskimos (more correctly Inuit but I didn't know that then) left their elderly to freeze to death. I believe that is most likely false.

It is felt by some neurologists that actual lack of empathy is mental disorder which can be seen on MRI scans as a change or decrease in grey matter. While somewhat controversial and extraordinarily challenging to treat, the main characteristic of Narcissistic Personality Disorder (NPD) is absence of empathy. Currently, the feeling is that approximately 1% of people have NPD. They have even seen changes on MRI is people with NPD. Genomic studies indicate that NPD was associated with polymorphisms in the serotonin transporter gene *(5-HTTLPR)*, and polymorphisms in the gene coding for the catabolic enzyme monoamine oxidase A (MAOA) involved in the regulation of biogenic amines like serotonin, norepinephrine, and dopamine, but not polymorphisms in the gene coding for the serotonin 5-HT2A receptor." (Dialogues Clin Neurosci. 2010 Mar; 12(1): 103–114). It has also developed in previously empathetic people post brain injury.

I can't find the source now but I have read that the higher up you go in organizations, the higher the percentage of people with NPD. So, the people at the bottom who do the actual work and don't get fairly paid for it are much "nicer" than the overpaid people at the top.

I once went to an exhibit on Neanderthals with my nephew (who doesn't believe in evolution but that's a whole different story!) at the Smithsonian. It was fascinating but the thing that emotionally affected me the most was the severely damaged leg bone of a male Neanderthal. The fact that the leg bone showed years of healing proved that this individual had been fed and cared for by his group for many years. The exhibit said there was no way he could have borne weight on those bones. There is no way he could have been hunting or gathering on his own. A group of Neanderthals had empathy and cared for a severely injured individual for years. Also, he had been carefully buried with grave goods which I think indicates that they valued him.

I used to spend a lot of time reading about and watching gorillas, orangutans, chimpanzees and bonobos. Researchers followed groups for months and identified individuals and tracked their activities. Often, I would see or read about empathetic actions to fellow primates who were not their offspring. For instance, I recall one episode was about an elderly female who fell. Later, necropsy showed she had broken her spine. The group stayed with her and brought her food until she died, although she was not a benefit to individual in the group. This makes me believe that clearly, the genetic routes for empathy are quite deep.

So, while I feel that empathy can have a dark side (as is often seen in Go-Fund-Me!) overall, it is a benefit to society as a whole. I view it as similar to the fact that Americans spend a ton of money on pet food and veterinary care while children go hungry. Does that mean loving pets has a dark side? Perhaps. Overall, I think in moderation, care for pets is good. I tend to think one wouldn't spend that veterinarian money on hungry children anyway. So why not support veterinarians? I think they tend to be extraordinarily empathetic.

———

While empathy can be described as self-serving, I do believe that most of the time, it comes from the heart. Empathy grows out a place of concern and wanting to relieve a person of suffering. If we choose not to try to connect and assist people in their greatest time of need, I think we do a disservice to humankind. Each of us will need assistance at some point, whether it's a kind word, a financial loan, a tutor for a subject not mastered, etc. In the examples given, building a house for someone who has suffered great loss may deny an opportunity to a laborer but in the case of massive destruction, there is much to be done and much assistance is needed. So, providing housing for a few would take only a few opportunities away from the laborer. As for the homeless person potentially using money given to them for drugs, etc., I figure it's up to them what they choose to do with the money that is given. We can only be responsible for providing what is believed to be help to those in need. Can you imagine what would have happened to this nation if the subsistence programs were not developed in response to the "Great Depression?" Thousands of people fell on hard times during this time and the assistance programs gave opportunities to those most in need.

———

To what degree are we responsible for the impacts of our empathetically-driven actions? For example, if you build a house in Haiti, are you depriving a Haitian laborer the opportunity to earn wages? Similarly, if you give a homeless person money and he uses it for drug, are you financing a bad, illegal, and dangerous action?

I think there are two different themes represented in this question. One theme is whether there is a correlation between your empathetic actions and the choices that others have the free will to make. If you give a homeless person money, you don't get the right to judge their behavior. That takes you down the path of whether it's appropriate to drug test people before giving them food stamps. To me, when you are offering help to someone, you shouldn't be doing it with strings tied to your own morality or judgments about how the person came to be in need.

The house building in Haiti question to me is a little different. That is more the question of whether or not you are putting your own time and energy into a project is more or less valuable then putting just your financial value into a project. I think there is a lot of personal growth that can come from putting your own time and energy into an empathetic project. I hope that comes out as a benefit somewhere down the road.

Alternatively, the world is full of well-intentioned empathy that has gone terribly wrong.

———

Following up on last round's discussion on nuclear energy as a critical component of a rational global climate change solution, the following Dilbert cartoon captures this well. Dilbert tells his boss: *"I invented a new type of nuclear power that has zero risk. It can be built in one day for less than a thousand dollars and it can power a small city"*. Dilbert's boss yells at him: *"GET THAT THING OUT OF HERE!"* and Dilbert leaves saying: *"I expect it will be hard to sell."*

———

I liked the 1955 Readers Digest definition of empathy in the "Short History of Empathy": *The ability to appreciate the other person's feelings without yourself becoming so emotionally involved that your judgment is affected."* I think this effectively responds to Paul Bloom's criticism of empathy as a misguided emotional response that favors tribal instincts. I don't disagree with Paul Bloom's notion that we would be better off using dispassionate rationalism when we make decisions that impact ourselves and others. I don't think empathy and rational decision-making are mutually exclusive. In fact, I continue to believe that empathy may be the critical component to our ability to survive and to achieve our individual and collective purpose.

As the interviewer asked in his discussion with Paul Bloom, in the absence of some common agreement that there is value in the lives of each human being, things like eugenics become logically persuasive techniques.

I came up with the set-up questions below to try to figure out whether it is our emotional or logical parts of the brain that make these decisions:

1. Do I care strongly about the welfare of all of my fellow human beings?
2. Do I care strongly about the welfare of a subset of my fellow human beings? (fellow countrymen, people who adhere to my religion, people in my local geographic locale, etc.)
3. Do I primarily feel strongly about the welfare of my immediate family and friends?
4. Do I primarily feel strongly about my own welfare?

It seems to me all of these are emotional rather than logically-derived views.

It seems like #1 is desirable, both from a societal and personal perspective: if we care about each other, we probably would have less problems.

#2 seems like a view that can be easily exploited by marketers, governments, and ideologies. We should carefully examine any actions or views that come from a standpoint of "us versus them."

#3 seems like a necessary viewpoint. We can and should focus our ourselves, our families, and our friends. Our capitalist system, which I believe is one of the most powerful and unstoppable forces in the world, relies on this being a dominant viewpoint. Such a viewpoint is necessary for us to get through the "survival stage" of our lives (making a living and supporting a family).

#4 is probably where most of us spend most of our time. I think that's been evolutionarily selected otherwise we would die of starvation if we kept giving our food away to hungry people. I think the challenge of our civilization is to train ourselves to develop more of an orientation for #1. I think the way to do that is to train ourselves to be more empathic while recognizing and watching out for the negative characteristics that inevitably come from emotionally-based feelings.

––––

I saw this on Paul's facebook page: *"Our lord has written the promise of resurrection, not in books alone, but in every leaf in springtime"* (MLK)

I really like that quote. It puts the resurrection in the context of a repetitive process: God continues to send his Son, who dies and is resurrected. It also takes it out of the metaphysical, not so much as a miraculous divine intervention but as part of an ongoing constant presence. The quote also reinforces my growing view that Jesus's role was as a messenger or a reminder of our purpose and direction, and did not intend to make himself the source of worship. From a standpoint of empathy, I think we should all focus on developing sense of empathy for ourselves and others - we are part of resurrection and the glory of nature - cultivate an empathic feeling of our connection to each other in something really important and glorious.

———

Since listening to Daniel Goldman's "Ted Talk" about giving money to panhandlers, I have thought about this a lot. For the Super Bowl, my family put together about 20 packages that included a five-dollar bill, a protein bar, a quote or joke, and scratch off lotto ticket (which triggered a debate on the appropriateness of state sponsored gambling, but that's a different topic) to give to panhandlers. I'm embarrassed to say that I have not actually given one of these packs to a panhandler since I never seem to have them with me when I can use them. However, two days ago, I walked into a 7-11 and there were two men out front. The first guy asked me for some money and I told him I didn't have any cash (which I didn't) so he asked if I could buy him an orange juice, which I said I would. The other guy then asked me if I could get him a slice of pizza and I agreed. While I was in the store, at the register, another guy asked me if I could buy him a pack of Marlborough lights, to which I said no. I later had a great discussion with my friend Dan about this. I think we came to the conclusion that there is no "right" answer to whether to give money to someone who asks but examining our thoughts and actions may be an important and useful thing to do. What made me buy these two guys orange juice and pizza when most of the time, I probably would have tried to avoid eye and ear contract? There were probably a bunch several factors involved including my knowing I'd have to walk by them again on the way out of the store; that I'm working on this empathy project; why did I buy orange juice (something healthy) and pizza (not so healthy) but not cigarettes (very not healthy)? I think I can say my decision to not buy the cigarettes was probably more related to the price rather than a judgment on the health risks of tobacco and to the fact that I he was the third person to ask me to buy something.

I just re-listened to the podcast with Daniel Goldman and think it's very good: *"Why aren't we more compassionate"* (TED Radio Hour) (12/19/2014)

———

Here's something I learned. Empathy sells! Advertisers have found that commercials that appeal to our sense of empathy have much more impact (do you remember the commercial of the American Indian crying in the "Keep America Beautiful" campaign?). Additionally, in the business world, executives who can convey a sense of empathy are more successful.

I think that makes Paul Bloom's thesis that we should not strive to cultivate empathy as a virtue somewhat moot. Perhaps empathy is neither a virtue or a vice but regardless of what it is, it "sells" and for both positive things and negative things.

Thinking a bit more broadly about advertising, I had the thought, "can we promote empathy or compassion or some other agreed upon value through advertising?" The answer is yes. I asked several people in the advertising business while researching this topic. There were a lot of articles on how to use empathy to sell products and a smaller number of articles on public service programs for things like smoking, drunk driving, etc. Campaigns of this sort were generally very successful.

In the run-up to the 2016 elections, we saw that Russian hackers and others were similarly successful in "advertising" discord by exploiting Americans' racial, economic, and cultural fears. Why can't we use advertising to promote more generalized viewpoints such as openness to other cultures, skepticism of misleading information, empathy, compassion, "we are in it together" orientation, etc.?

You might ask, "who is going to pay for this? If we consider the amount of money that large donors contributed to politicians, AND if you consider that some portion of these large donors did so for altruistic purposes, AND you assume that half of those donors get no return on their "investment" (because their candidate loses), wouldn't some portion of those donors be willing to pool their funds into a "empathy" advertising campaign? It might be that you could get bi-partisan support for some areas (although off the top of my head I can't think what that might be).

Similarly, we are in the age of "Giving Pledge" and Philanthrocapitalism (which is rich businessmen who give money to charity but are involved in how that money is spent). For all the money that is spent on health and education - isn't there a case to be made for spending money on promoting compassion?

Our brains are wired to make decisions based on emotions rather than logic. It is easy to say that we should de-emphasize the emotion (empathy) for the logical (Utilitarianism) but that's not how we are built.

I like the quote by zoologist and surrealist painter Desmond Morris:

"*I view my fellow man not as a fallen angel, but as a risen ape.*" From a standpoint of evolution, we are a very early work in progress in terms of treating each other with logical compassion. In the meantime, I believe empathy, combined with self-awareness of the biases involved in emotional feelings, is the way to go.

Want to check Desmond Morris's artwork? Google *"Desmond Morris The Old Dilemma"*.

———

Based on our further venturing into this topic, here's what I understand to be empathy and compassion:

Empathy is an emotion originating in the supramarginal gyrus part of the cerebral cortex. Empathy is triggered by "mirror" neurons based on observational stimuli and create the sensation of experience the feelings of another sentient or non-sentient thing.

Empathy is the primary emotion that allows humans to bond into a social order and to feel compassion for each other.

From a societal standpoint, compassion is the value we should strive for. How does one foster a sense of compassion in oneself and help foster compassion in others? There may be two ways: fostering empathy and fostering rationally based arguments why we should "care" about each other.

Fostering empathy is challenging because it can easily result in association with tribalism and other "us versus them" motivations. Because the emotion focuses on "what I see in front of me," it does not translate well into public policy or meaningful solutions.

Fostering rationally based arguments why we should care about each other make sense but it probably isn't effective in terms of changing our culture. We make decisions based on emotions and we vote for the candidate that we would "most like to have a beer with."

So, at this point, I believe that fostering empathy in ourselves and in others is the most effective way at this point in bridging our growing gap between democrats and republicans, Muslims vs Judeo/Christians, Coastals vs Heartlands, the hyper-rich versus working Americans vs persons in poverty, etc., etc.

——-

To what degree are we responsible for the impacts of our empathetically-driven actions? For example, if you build a house in Haiti, are you depriving a Haitian laborer the opportunity to earn wages? Similarly, if you give a homeless person money and he uses it for drug, are you financing a bad, illegal, and dangerous action?

Riffing on the prompt above…

I absolutely believe that we are responsible for our impact on others. In fact, the ability to do just that is an important character trait that most of us overlook at best, and completely fail to develop at worst. It's an overlooked leadership skill whether you are acting as a member of your immediate family or as an employee in a multi-million dollar enterprise. That's just awareness of your impact on others, not your actual impact, good or bad. However, I think that your impact on others is a bit different than the impacts of our empathetically-driven actions. Empathetic actions are a choice. You choose to do them. Sometimes you are empathetic but stop short of action. Sometimes you take action but it turns into problem solving rather than an action of empathy. I suspect that it's tough for some to make the distinction – it is for me. Other times, I am greatly aware of the empathetic action I could take, but I don't. I'm too emotionally drained and wrapped up in my own world and the problems in it.

I feel guilty. So, I turn to other means. I keep those people in my thoughts and I pray for them when I wish I could do more but lack the strength to move to action. Perhaps that is enough. Perhaps I will do more when I can. I think that's where it ends up for most people: do what you can but don't feel guilty about what you cannot control. There will be times in life where you will be on the receiving end of empathetically-driven actions and times when you need to give to those in need of empathy. The truth is we have far too many people in our lives to exhaust or focus our capability to be empathetic. We do what we can and we use our experience and judgement to practice empathy – it's not perfect but better than nothing.

———

We were encouraged to read Paul Bloom's essay in The Atlantic about a darker side of empathy. In my opinion, he writes wisely…"*I'm not usually in favor of killing but I'd make an exception for the killers of ISIS. During my better moments, I acknowledge that what I really want is for them (ISIS) to stop torturing and killing people; that any violent act towards them should be judged on its probable consequences: how much it makes the world better, how it deters these sorts of acts in the future rather than on how satisfying it might be to me or my friends. Everyone appreciates that fear and hate can motivate ugly choices; we should be mindful that our most tender sentiments do the same.*" (The Atlantic)

To the extent that we feel deep empathy for someone who has been hurt and wronged, we tend to strike out against the ones who did the hurting. However, striking out impulsively is a form of tribalism . . . us vs. them. Our own aggression, even though driven by empathy, tends to escalate the violence and hatred and divisiveness in the world. How can that help in any deep or meaningful way? I agree with Bloom that our empathy, though essential, must be tempered by thoughtful consideration and by principles, e.g., every person has value and worth, especially those who seem most "different." Gandhi, in his soul-searching struggle for social justice, came to the same conclusion and his non-violent protest became known throughout the world.

To what degree are we responsible for the impacts of our empathy-driven actions? I believe that we are responsible for thinking about the possible repercussions of what we choose to do. It might feel good to give money to the homeless person who is right before me but might it be better to give that money to a shelter that provides food and beds and health care? It would be intellectually lazy and self-indulgent to simply hand over money directly to a panhandler and feel like, "now I've done my part." It is better to try to really "see" the suffering person in front of you and do the hard work of trying to discern how best to help. Just like the question of whether volunteer work in Haiti might deprive Haitian laborers a chance to work, there are no easy answers. Empathic *feelings* might lead to impulsive actions that may hurt more than help. In a deep sense, we must learn to bear the weight of not being *sure* that we've done the best thing. We can only hope that the actions that flow from our desire to help *do* make the world a better place.

Round Four: Empathy and Technology

Here was the prompt:

Hi all! I hope you enjoyed round three! Since people liked this topic, let's get more adventurous and tackle the challenging and interesting topic of empathy and technology.

Here are a couple articles for your consideration and one podcast:

- *"Empathy technologies like VR, AR, and social media can transform education"* (Jennifer Carolan: Techcrunch 4/22/18)

- *"AI Challenge: Achieving Artificial Empathy"* (Lisa Morgan: Information Week 4/25/18)

- *"Empathy is the key to great marketing campaigns"* (Abhilash Patel: Forbes 4/14/18)

- Empathy In AI with Rob Walker podcast (TWIML 4/5/19)

There are so many great questions and topics for discussion around this very broad topic of empathy and technology. Of course, feel free to develop your thoughts on anything related to this topic. The following are suggested prompts only:

- To what degree do social media, connected devices (smart phones and tablets), video games, and voice services (like Alexa) impact our sense of empathy?

- What might be some of the impacts of artificial intelligence on our sense of empathy?
- Can we/should we program empathy into our technologies?

Grandes cosas por venir!

Responses:

In considering the dark side of technology, it's easy to identify areas of concern: violent gaming, bullying, intrusions of privacy, using sales techniques that lead to consumer debt, using drones to kill people. The list is endless. What is perhaps unique about technology and AI is the rapidity and the power they command. Just as ancient battles were fought hand-to-hand and resulted in relatively fewer deaths, today's warfare has the capacity to destroy most of the human life on the planet. I believe that it is essential to think in advance about how we want or don't want to use our technology. Just because we can do something doesn't mean that we should do it. With CRISP-R technology, is it good to "design" human babies? Who makes the decisions? Who should make the decisions? Who IS making the decisions? It is tempting to become overwhelmed with the complexity of determining the ethical challenges and not think about them but that wouldn't help anyone.

"*Attention is the beginning of devotion.*" (Mary Oliver) She, of course, was talking about attention to nature, including all creatures. A terrible consequence, sometimes, of screen devotion is that it robs us of the ability to pay attention to the world that immediately surrounds us. Attention is finite and, whatever focus is directed toward technology, that much less is available to attending with empathy to the world around us.

—

This concept of "artificial empathy" is of particular interest to me. My job requires me to be empathetic. Most of the time I truly am empathetic. But, on rare occasions-headache, exhaustion, stress over other issues, I must "fake empathy." Like the actors in the Jennifer Carolan article, I have to "act" empathetic even though I just don't feel empathetic. I guess I know "my lines" and what tone of voice to use? Generally, I think and truly hope, I am perceived as genuine. Basic Good Manners and ethics can cover a lot too!

The other statement from Carolan's article that I found profound was "social media platforms once held so much promise to connect us all in an online utopia. The reality is that social media has moved us in the opposite direction. Instead, our platforms have us caught in an echo chamber of our own social filters, rarely exposed to new perspectives."

To what degree do social media, connected devices (smart phones and tablets), video games, and voice services (like Alexa) impact our sense of empathy? I wonder if anyone has read the book "Ready Player One?" My nephew recommended it to me. It is a fabulous book that made me think and gave me a different perception on the value of video games and on-line friendships. It is set in a dystopic 2044. There is no actual physical contact between people, only via computers. Even high school is online. Teenager Wade Watts only ever interacts with others using his avatar Parzival. The world is miserable so people try to spend any free time in an online virtual reality world called Oasis. Oasis is free and was created by a kind man named James Halliday who is now dead. But a superrich evil company called IOI is trying to take control of Oasis and monetize it. Without Oasis, all poor people's lives would be far more unpleasant.

James Halliday hid an Easter Egg inside Oasis and the first person who finds it will inherit/control Oasis. There is a desperate, deadly competition between Parzival and IOI to find this Easter Egg. He competes with and later joins forces with Art3mis who is also trying to find the Easter Egg. Their relationship grows and develops entirely online. They join forces and work together to save Oasis from IOI.

To make a long, exceptionally exciting story short, Wade finally meets Artemis. Her real name is Samantha and you realize the benefit of all their previous interactions having been purely online. Samantha has a large birth defect on her face. If Wade had met her in person, this birth defect would have probably precluded him from ever being interested in her. But because Wade has fallen in love with Samantha's inner self online instead of having been turned off by her outer appearance, he realizes that loves Samantha regardless of her appearance.

I don't have a voice service but the ones I've heard don't sound empathetic; they sound robotic. It would probably be nice, albeit possibly creepy, to make Alexa or whoever seem more empathetic.

What might be some of the impacts of artificial intelligence on our sense of empathy? I think it is possible making computer programs seem more empathetic might make people who spend a lot of time online act more empathetic in their world view. I don't think the research exists to demonstrate it but some people certainly feel that playing violent video games makes kids be more violent. Perhaps interacting with more empathetic computer programs might make people more empathetic. Abhilash Patel's article on empathy being the key to good marketing campaigns cited a study that supported that concept.

Can we/should we program empathy into our technologies? I don't know if we can. Lisa Morgan's commentary on Artificial Empathy pointed out that a machine understanding a human's emotions is not the same as empathizing with a human's emotions. If we can, I think we probably should, not to increase sales but to foster a general increase in empathy in our society.

It's not AI, but Roy Rogers sent me an ad on a Friday saying, "*You worked really hard this week and you deserve a pleasant Roy Rogers' meal.*" Frankly, I had worked really hard and lots of extra hours that week and it didn't seem like anyone appreciated my hard work until I got that email from Roy Rogers. They also made me feel good about being a mom the Friday before Mother's Day. I didn't go out and buy a Double R Bar Burger either week (more of a roast beef and horseradish person), but they did somehow make me feel a little good about myself. I'm sure they hope will translate into buying Roy Rogers at some point (and probably will). Edible Arrangements and the Oncology Nursing Society try to do something similar but don't actually make me feel good about myself.

Abhilash Patel's marketing article seems to give social media credit for the increasing empathy that Americans have for the LGBTQ community. I am not sure that is true but, if so, it does indicate that there is a benefit to programing empathy into technology.

—

I think I'll tackle 1 and 3 together. I think the empathy that comes from social media is a little impersonal and fake. It can be real but the largest gigantic percentage of it is people just complaining. There are some very powerful advertising campaigns out there. None of these things make me feel like I want to buy whatever products though. And don't get me started on the Humane Society adds with the abused animals. I understand that it could be a good fundraising tactic but the emotional trauma we all endure watching the ad is too much. I think empathy should be reserved for person to person contact. I don't want Alexa trying to console me about things.

—

As a "tech guy," Paul was right. This topic is quite interesting to me. I see both the positives and negatives that these technologies bring to our society. It's exciting yet scary. I'm not a heavy user on social media, although I do have a presence on several of the platforms including Facebook. I guess you'd say, I'm more of a voyeur than a creator. Social media gives us a window into the lives of others unlike the more limited view that we have with close friends and family. Social media gives people the ability to express emotion through their posts and online interactions. This, in turn, gives us the opportunity to practice empathy via a better understanding of the emotional state that others are presenting online. Notice that I deliberately said an understanding of the emotional state that others are "presenting."

What you see on social media is not real. It's not the whole story. It's incomplete and easy to misinterpret. We view our broader social media circle through a lens that is determined by the person who is posting. They choose what to post and how to present it. How to spin it. It's filtered. Furthermore, it's next to impossible to truly understand the emotion behind the post. Sure, you might be able to ascertain that someone is sad when they post about the loss of a parent but you can't tell how sad or how that emotion may be impacting the individual. Were they really close to their parents? Were they estranged? Did they pass unexpectedly or did they live a good, long life? How does that impact someone else's life moving forward? There are an infinite number of degrees of emotion and thus an infinite spectrum of opportunities for empathy. It's hard to interpret through the lens of social media.

I think that social media increases our awareness of others and presents many opportunities to express empathy, which is good, but I also believe that our capability and capacity to practice empathy fluctuates over time. Sometimes we can give a lot and sometimes we have little to give. Because I have 300 "friends" on social media, does that mean I need to be aware of the emotional state of 300 people and respond empathetically to all of them? What if I am emotionally drained and need more empathy than I can give? We have limited capacity for empathy as it peaks and valleys over the years. The developers of social media and technologies like Alexa stand to benefit from developing the UIs with what appears to be empathic technology but the truth is that humans are far too complex and the programming won't get it right all the time. Some people cry when they are afraid, others laugh. (Ever been to a haunted house)? How can you tell the difference, without deep context, between a person's emotional state and patterns of behavior?

I guess that brings us to AI. I generally cringe whenever I hear of AI. Many companies talk up AI and machine learning because buzzwords sell products but what they are really talking about is pattern recognition. You can program a computer to make an assumption about an individual's emotional state based on facial expressions, behavior tracking, search history and the context of one's network but this is something that humans often get wrong so how can we expect a computer to get it right. It's far too complex and far too nuanced. Empathy is more complex. I'm not saying that AI doesn't have a place here but we're just far from anything that could be viable and trusted. As companies continue to develop capabilities, we'll see more and more use of AI to read a person's emotional state and make an attempt at empathy – to connect with a customer on that level – but it's still a guess and there are risks associated with misinterpretation. Anyway, I think that AI might have potential positive applications but mostly would serve to increase our awareness of opportunities to practice empathy. With this increased awareness, will we all have increased capacity for empathy? Probably not. Or, perhaps AI will replace the need to be empathic altogether, relieving the emotional burden on humans, but I doubt we'll see that in our lifetime. For example, remember that high school friend that you haven't talked to in years? Well, their mother passed away and they are devastated. The algorithm sees this happening in your network and sends a nice note of condolence. You never need to see that note because the AI took care of it for you... ☺

I can understand why we might want to program empathy into our technologies. It's just very far-fetched to think that we will get there in a meaningful way anytime soon. We've barely mastered pattern recognition and that's not even AI. Besides, emotion is uniquely human (ok, animals, too). It's infinitely complex and something that a machine doesn't need. Computers aren't happy or sad and even if they were, they'd still do what they're programmed to do. People do have emotions and we practice empathy in reaction to the emotions and situations of other humans and animals. For us, it's a need. We need emotion, we live and die by it. It is part of our nature.

Social media and technologies like AI certainly can influence our interpretations of emotion and raise our level of awareness when it comes to empathy but technology is but one of many influences our complex world. It will present opportunities but also many challenges as we view and interact with our world through technology that doesn't always get it right. Algorithms make mistakes too.

—

Have we become digital zombies?

Like most people, I have very mixed feelings about technology's impact on what it means to be a "purposeful" human. When I say purposeful, I think purpose comes through introspection and interactions with other people or other living things and taking actions in accordance with this introspection and interactions.

Overall, I think technology has had a positive impact on my interactions. When my daughters were off to school for four years, I could easily communicate with them by text or facetime. Some say that communication via text or other electronic means is not the same "quality" as more traditional communications, but I think I disagree with that; the quality of the communication is up to us.

I do think though, that technology can magnify certain traits and activities at the cost of others. On Mothers' Day, I walked through the eatery at the Mall around the lunch hour. Of the people who were by themselves, the vast majority were on their cell phones. Of the people who were there with others, I would say over half of them were on their phones. I saw one family - mother father and three children in a round booth - all on their phones. I had this thought that maybe zombies aren't hideous creatures who walk slowly and try to eat humans; maybe zombies are people who have been "eaten" by their cell phones.

I had an argument with my spouse. We were driving somewhere and she was on her phone the whole time. I asked her what she was doing. She said she was going through her emails; her personnel email gets clogged with thousands of email advertisements and she needs to go through them and delete the ones she doesn't "need." When I told her that if we are together on a car ride, it would be nice to talk and interact with each other instead of me being the driver and she being in her own digital world. She replied that I was similarly on my phone "all the time" and if I wanted to talk, what would I like to talk about? Of course, at that moment I couldn't think of a "topic" to talk about and she went back to her emails.

This experience made me think about a couple things. If we spend a lot of our time online, does it matter what we are doing online? Is internet shopping, consuming advertising, porn, gambling, or celebrity gossip a "bad" use of our time while writing this essay or learning about global warming a "good" use of our time? Also, if we live in our separate digital worlds and need a "discussion topic" to reenter a human interaction, what do we miss along the way?

Digital distractions are obviously here to stay. I think that to avoid becoming "digital zombies," we will have to come up with disciplines to stay connected to the non-digital world. This might include digital-device-enforced quiet periods or digital tools to teach/guide us to have interactions with other humans.

—

I just finished reading Michelle Obama's book "Becoming". I thought the last two sentences were really beautiful and apropos to the broader topic of empathy.

> *"And there's grace in being willing to know and hear others. This, for me, is how we become."*

First off, I really like sentences that start with the word "and." I remember a teacher in grade school circling in red a sentence I had written and writing "you can't start a sentence with "And."

Yes, you can! Childhood school traumas aside, I love the idea that there is something mystically rewarding (grace) that derives from listening (hearing others), and "know" others (having empathy) and that, moreover, is both the secret to the path and to the designation; "becoming" by listening and coming to know others.

I think this writing project is, in some small way, a way of "being willing to know and hear others" - so keep it up team!

—

Where is the orange juice?

I try to think strategically about what line to get into, especially grocery stores. Sometimes the shorter line is not the fastest one. I usually look to see what lines the "regulars" use, assuming they know which is the fastest line. I was at a Safeway yesterday and got into a line with just one person. I was distracted by a podcast that I was listening to and after dumping my stuff on the conveyer belt, the grocery checker was engaged in a discussion with the woman. With mild irritation, I pulled my ear buds off to find out what was the problem. The checker, who looked like the late comedian Dick Gregory, was telling the woman how beautiful she was and she was beaming from ear to ear. When she finally left, he greeted me with *"How are you today young man?"* I told him that I thought he had made the woman's day and he said that he could tell that she was feeling bad and wanted to make her feel better.

"It's a choice, you know that, right?" he asked me. A woman and her friend walked up behind me, said, *"Excuse me, where is the orange juice?"* To which the checker replied, *"In the orange."* The lady, her friend, and I thought about that for a few seconds and then the lady and her friend started laughing and she rephrased her question: *"Where are the bottles of orange juice?"* He stepped out from behind the cash register and walked the women to the orange juice section, returning a few minutes later to finish up the transaction. As he handed me the receipt, he said something very encouraging, something about about how important it was to be a "good man" in today's society.

He was extraordinary. I imagine that this man has hundreds of meaningful interactions with people every day. If there's a spectrum of being about to read emotions and make meaningful connections, this person must be at another level than most of us.

That's what it's all about, I think.

———-

"Fiction is empathy technology" (Steven Pinker)

I saw this quote in one of my Google searches for "Empathy and technology." I don't totally know what it means, but I wrote it down and it stuck on me.

And here's why:

First, in researching the topic of empathy, I have learned that imagination is a critical component. If you can't imagine how someone else perceives or feels, you can't empathize with them. I had never thought of it this way. If that's that case, I have a sense that we tend to have a greater sense of imagination and wonder when we are younger and that life tends to limit our sense of imagination. Every day we age, more doors close than open and we better see the limitations of ourselves, others, and us collectively.

Also, I have a sense that as a society, our collective imagination may be decreasing. Growing up playing outdoors or drawing with blank paper and crayons fosters imagination. Similarly, the act of reading or being read to causes us to transform the words into images. My sense is that children today spend a lot more time playing video games that might foster certain skills but probably not imagination. I also think that watching a video is probably not the same from the standpoint of fostering imagination as translating the written or spoken word in our minds. I'm reminded of the beginning of the Gospel of John, "In the beginning was the Word" (not "In the beginning was a streaming video after a twenty second ad").

Continuing, technology is defined as *"the application of scientific knowledge for practical purposes."* I don't understand how fiction can be considered technology but thinking about it a bit more broadly, technology might be considered methodology for achieving an objective. So, a cotton gin is a technology that separates cotton fibers from the seeds and greatly increased the efficiency of the cotton industry. Similarly, if we consider "Empathy" to be a critical emotion that needs to be enhanced for the well-being of our species, then story-telling (i.e. fiction) is critical to the development of empathy.

I don't think that's the best interpretation of Steven Pinker's quote but thinking about it and trying to articulate my thoughts did give me a better insight into the importance of imagination and story-telling as techniques for better understanding ourselves and others.

Interestingly (or sadly), the cotton gin was instrumental in the institutionalization of slavery, according to the Encyclopedia Britannica, *"The simplicity of the invention—which could be powered by man, animal, or water—caused it to be widely copied despite Whitney's patent; it is credited with fixing cotton cultivation, virtually to the exclusion of other crops, in the U.S. South and so institutionalizing slavery."*

———-

Do people only read things if title promises an apocalyptic future?

I came across a really interesting article: <u>*"Is Technology Destroying Empathy"*</u> (Live Science)

The writer, PJ Manney, makes several interesting observations which have been covered in previous rounds of this writing project but I liked the way she described them:

- Describing how empathy does not work well outside of our immediate network: *"Our brains' empathy systems have their share of problems. Most humans are generally good at empathizing with individuals but we're not so good at trying to do the same for an entire nation or ethnic group."*

- Referencing the study "War Play," how can the emotion of empathy be manipulated? In the study, the U.S. military has used video game technology to suppress empathy in soldiers. Additionally, she cites ideological information *"silos of broadcast, print, website and social media, where conservatives or liberals only listen, read, and watch their own thoughts repeated in recursive echo chambers of increasingly radical and exclusionary thought."*

- The notion that technology is neither "pro or anti" empathy; it can be a tool to either foster or impair empathy. She cites things the quick change in opinion in the Western world on same sex marriage powered by social media; Verona, a dating app that pairs Israelis with Palestinians by bypassing religious views and matching people based on commonalities based on questions such as "What are you most passionate about?" Additionally, she references Chris Milk's Ted Talk: *"How Virtual Reality Can Create the Ultimate Empathy Machine."* In this TED talk,

Chris Milk posits that: "*It connects humans to other humans in a profound way that I've never seen before in any other form of media. And it can change people's perception of each other. And that's who I think virtual reality has the potential to actually change the world.*"

It's an interesting perspective. I guess I think of virtual reality as a new and more powerful way for people to disengage from interaction with other living people but if we can use it to "*Create the Ultimate Empathy Machine,*" let's do it!

———

While technology is without a doubt a benefit to the human race, I think there are times, improperly used, when it can isolate us from humanity and harden our hearts. I am sure other commentators will explore those social pathologies better than I can. I propose to take my thoughts on a different path. I offer what Pope Francis has called the Theology of Tears. For example, in 2016 as part of the Holy Year of Mercy, the Pope scheduled a prayer vigil "to dry the tears" of those who are weeping, inviting parents who have lost a child, victims of war and torture, the seriously ill, the desperate, those enslaved by addiction and everyone else in need of consolation.

"*Sometimes, tears are the only true response to the question of why the innocent suffer.*" I am impressed by the eloquence of one of his statements: "*Certain realities of life,*" he said, "*are seen only with eyes that are cleansed by tears.*" Pope Francis continued: "*For people who are safe, comfortable and loved, learning how to weep for others is part of following Jesus, who wept at the death of Lazarus and was moved with compassion at the suffering of countless others.*"

John 11:35 says "Jesus wept." In most Bible versions, this is the shortest verse but very powerful, very compassionate words. Tears usually come to us in times of great joy and great sadness. I would argue that if a person has never experienced tears of sadness or joy, that person has lived a life without connection to humanity and has not experienced true empathy.

Important points to make here are the general definitions of Apathy, Sympathy and Empathy.

- Apathy: means that you don't feel anything. It is the opposite of love. In some cases, I think it might be a worse emotion to have in regard to other people than hate.
- Sympathy: you feel sorry for a person and perhaps you make a pledge to donate money to a cause.
- Empathy: true empathy drives a person to perform a conscious and deliberate act to help alleviate suffering. In my mind, empathy is the most noble and constructive act a person can perform to show true love.

In summary, tears demonstrate that have experienced love and appreciate the plight of those not as fortunate as us and that we empathize with human suffering

Round 5: Our Relationship with Animals

Hi everybody, this month's discussion is on empathy as seen through the lens of our relationships to other living things (aka anthro-zooology). Below were the prompts and responses. I hope you find them interesting:

- What does our relationship to animals (there's a word for it: "anthrozoology") tell us about ourselves? Is it a problem (for our collective society) when we care for our pets more than other humans?
- What are the ethical, empathetic, and environmental implications of eating animals
- What responsibility should we have for the treatment of animals (in the wild and in captivity)
- How does the anthropomorphism of animals relate to empathy?
- How do you feel about the concept of "Speciesism"? (defined as "a form of discrimination based on species membership. It involves treating members of one species as morally more important than members of other species even when their interests are equivalent. More precisely, speciesism is the failure to consider interested of equal strength to an equal extent because of the species of which the individuals are a member." (wiki))

———

Responses:

Thoughts on Speciesism:

As I participated in the initial project about what we have learned so far, I came to realize that I deeply believe that all creation is interdependent and interconnected. The definition of speciesism as treating members of one species as morally more important than members of another species is interesting and evocative. On one hand I can easily someone ridiculing the idea that worms are as valuable as humans. But, at a deep level, I think this is true. We are, all of us, made of stardust. But, for the sake of simplicity, let's consider larger animals (dogs, cats, elephants, whales, etc.). Karen Armstrong, in her meditation on the true meaning of the Golden Rule, asks us to look into our own hearts, discover what gives us pain, and then refuse, under any circumstance whatsoever, to inflict that pain on anybody else. I would extend that "anyone else" to any creature capable of feeling pain. And so I hope that research using animals will stop. Already medical simulations are being used in medical training and technological advances likely can offer similar alternatives to animal experimentation. All of us have heard about the extinctions of so many species due to habitat loss, poaching, environmental degradation, etc. It's overwhelming to think of all that needs to be done.

Sometimes I wonder what future generations will look back on and consider barbaric/evil about our current society (the way we can look back and see blatant racism/sexism/misogyny in both our national and our religious history). I suspect that one condemnation will be the way we have failed to protect and respect animals.

A few personal experiences might be relevant here. One of the most thrilling moments of my life happened on a National Geographic whale- watching trip. A small group of us were in a zodiac out in the Gulf of California when we were startled by a huge whale looming high over us, looking intently at us with her huge eyes. Then she sank below the surface and, within a minute, her young calf emerged close by and spy- hopped over to us, allowing me to pat its head. Our guide believed that the mother inspected us, judged us to be safe, and then allowed her baby to learn something about humans.

Several years ago, our beloved golden retriever died and, in my grief, I sobbed that, *"if dogs don't go to heaven, then I don't want to either!"* I have come to completely believe that, whatever heaven is, all creation will share it.

I encourage people to watch a youtube video (type in "dog crying while watching the sad part of Lion King") and marvel at the dog's empathy. I suspect that everyone who has loved their pets know how empathic they can be. I also recommend watching Mama's Last Goodbye (that Paul recommended). So moving.

—

The topic of human's relationship to animals is one I actually think about regularly. And when I am in a conversation about what makes us special in the scope of our planet and even universe, it always seems to come back to animals. We like to believe that we a special species. There must be some reason why we are the dominant species on Earth, why we are the only creatures who are seemingly aware of ourselves and the universe around us, and why we alone are capable of destroying ourselves. No one questions how we are special compared to inanimate objects. No one feels bad when they throw a rock or they eat a potato. But most people certainly think it's wrong to kick a puppy. But where exactly is the line between what's okay to kick, what's okay to eat, and what's okay to experiment on? For the most part, people seem to draw those lines around- okay to kick anything other than an animal, okay to eat anything less conscious than a pig or cow, and okay to experiment on anything that is not human. But is there something so inherently different between a cow and a chimpanzee that makes one acceptable to eat and the other not? And what is the separation between a chimpanzee and a human that makes it okay to perform certain experiments on them but not humans? Everyone agrees that there is some difference between a slug, a cow, and a chimpanzee. That their worth and how we treat them is something of a scale based on how intelligent the animal is or how it seems to react to things. But would we ever be able to come up with a definition of how to treat animals? What is okay to do to a slug vs how we should treat chimpanzees? What is our measure, our formula? If everything is truly a scale, then how do we know that humans aren't just at the top of the scale? There's nothing special about us other than being at the top, we're just *slightly* more intelligent and we just feel *slightly* more than chimpanzees. Why are we the species tasked with being stewards for all other species? Is it just because we are the most intelligent, or is it because we are special? It would be nice if we could find one measure of how we are truly different from all other animals. I used to think it was the ability to be aware of our role in the world, but maybe it has to do with empathy. Are we in charge of all other species because we have the capacity to feel emotions towards them and each other? But then the real issue for me with this is that if we say we are special because we can be empathetic, then what does that mean for people with who can't feel empathy? Just because someone has a mental disorder or doesn't have the same feelings as someone else, does that mean they are less special or less human? I struggle to come up with something that sets all humans apart from all animals. Maybe there isn't one. Maybe it is just a continuous scale and there's nothing special about us. But then why should we care if we destroy a planet and all its living creatures? If some more intelligent alien species dropped down on our planet, would they treat us the same as we treat our animals and think it is justified?

—

OK, here are my thoughts before reading the materials.

The notion of speciesism is somewhat new to me but when I think about our relationship with animals, this concept opens up new ways to think about things. We naturally feel kinship for primates, I think because we recognize our similarities, pets, because we have created bonds, and "cute" animals (I think there should be an analog to "*survival of the fittest*" with "*survival of the cutest*".)

I have thought about the ethics of the meat industry for the past couple of years. I think of it in the context of environmentalism, the high cost of converting plant calories to meat calories, and the impact on the animals. I don't think I'm ready to become a vegetarian, but I definitely would like to reduce my intake of meat. I'd also be very willing to pay more for companies that would use more humane techniques for meat production. I tend to think the idea of the food chain and "circle of life" is built into this reality. I do think that animals that we eat do deserve our respect and that the distance we have from the production of the meat (and slaughter) is not a healthy thing.

After reading the materials, I have an increased appreciation for our fundamental similarity, and bond, with animals. The only way we can justify our treatment of animals is through false moral codes and ethics systems designed to justify actions that our emotional sense of empathy could not reconcile.

—

For as long as I can remember, animals have played an important role in my life. I grew up with at least one dog in the house – in fact – I can't remember ever living without one... ever. I'm sure that has shaped my views on animals in a positive way. I've always been around an array of animals, mostly pet fish, parakeets, and even hermit crabs over the years. No cats though, sorry.

And of course, a life lived into parent-hood has provided many opportunities for exposure to many more through visits to zoon, farms, aquariums and just generally living in the suburbs where we share our outdoor space with squirrels, birds, snakes, and bugs. I'm a carnivore as is my family, we like to fish (catch and release), I don't hunt nor do I have any desire to, and my views on animals are fluid and often complex and conflicting. It's something that you may not think about too often.

For example, I don't think twice about eating meat, but I don't like the idea of how it gets to my plate. I just don't think about it. What makes it ok to eat a cow, but we wouldn't think of eating dogs or horses? As for other cultures, I don't really take a position. I'm often quick to smash a bug that has invaded "my" space but other times I'll think twice about stomping a spider or I'll try to usher a fly out of the house rather than swatting it. Sometimes I just react without thinking and smash away. I like to see squirrels running around the yard, but rats are unwelcome. Animals and insects must think that human behavior is very strange.

One thing that I think our relationship with animals teaches us is that our feelings towards animals are as varied as they are towards other humans. And yes, that can be problematic. We are selective in our empathetic response depending on our relationship with each other, animals and humans alike. We can be dog lovers but cat haters. We are selective in the value we put on life. It may not have as much impact on the life of a fly or a small rodent as it does on another person, but I do believe that our relationship with animals does influence and shape our views on people – both people who are like us and people who are different. We tend to take care of our flock where it's easier to practice empathy, but we fall short when we don't like someone – or have preferences for one species, race, gender, culture over another. We simply don't direct much of our energy to the latter. We can shut off our emotions and reserve our empathy for only the people or animals that we choose.

How we treat animals can be a good indicator of how we treat people in general. I think it's especially important for children to learn about the ethical treatment of animals at an early age. It may even help with emotional development and build our capacity for empathy.

We, as humans, often treat each other like animals. That statement can have negative connotations, or it could be positive – it all depends on how we view and treat animals. Perhaps better understanding of how we view and treat animals of all kinds will lend itself well to developing our capacity and capability to treat our fellow humans ethically – with the kindness and empathy that we might otherwise reserve for our beloved pets. At the very least, this exercise in thinking about our relationship with animals, has increased my awareness of how I think about relationships with fellow humans. We choose our interactions and shape our relationships to others based on what we have learned growing up.

Sadly, I find myself writing and processing these thoughts directly on the heels of 3 mass shootings in the past week. It boggles the mind. How do we as humans have the capacity to do something so senseless and so inhumane? It's a rarity in the broader animal kingdom. I'd be interested to understand, from the perpetrator's perspective, how we as a species can sink so low. Is there a correlation between their views on the treatment of animals that leads to these despicable actions? After all, we are all animals.

I think humans have a lot to learn from animals and our relationships with them.

—

The NPR article "*Mama's Last Hug' Makes Case That Humans Are Not Alone In Experiencing Emotions*" book review of Franz De Waal's book: "Mama's Last Hug" made a convincing argument to me that human's are not unique or special in the experience of emotions. The connection between "Mama", the 59 year old chimpanzee and Jan van Hoof, as shown in the video shows this viscerally. I guess another argument that make human's unique is the notion of "consciousness" - I'd like to learn more about this, but I suspect that this is not a key differentiator - I have a growing notion that the concept of consciousness is an illusion that was evolutionarily helpful to the rise and domination of the human species - it allows us to justify almost anything.

An interesting point raised in the article is the topic of anthropomorphism - De Waal is not concerned about anthropomorphism - projecting our emotions on animals - he's worried about the opposite: anthropodenial, that we refuse to acknowledge our similarities because it would cause us to rethink our treatment of animals.

—

I spent some time on Google trying to find out what makes us different than all the other animals. Many of the things that we have previously thought are not true - animals have empathy, language, grieve the loss of their loved ones. One differentiator (at least so far) is that humans appear to be the only species that blushes. However, in my view, an important difference is that we have learned to write things down and with this power, can share knowledge much more efficiently than others. This power, however, also allows us to write things down that are immoral and call it inspired word. This understanding makes me realize that everything written down - scriptures, codes, laws, great books, all need to be questioned and challenged.

—

I am currently reading Dr Aysha Akhtar's book: *"Our Symphony with Animals"*. In a podcast, Dr Akhtar says: *"Developing our sense of kindness toward animals is so important for us as individuals and for us as a society and it's the only way we can exist and move forward as a species."* A similar point she makes is that our experience with pets is one of two way unconditional love. Having this experience fortifies us and helps us develop important skills as we go out into the world and interact with fellow human beings, which, even in the most loving and mutually dependent relationship, falls short of unconditional love. If you have a chance to read the book or listen to Dr Akhtar on an interview, I think you'll get some meaningful insights on our shared destiny with animals.

—

I saw a bumper sticker on a car (in the shape of a dog biscuit) that said "*My dog digs Camp Bow Wow*", which made me have a few thoughts that are hopefully relevant to the discussion:

It created an image of what sometimes seems conspicuous expense and attention paid to pets - like when people bequeath their multi-million dollar estates to their pets, like the $12 million slumlord Leona Helmsley bequest to her Maltese dog "*Trouble*" (see photo)

I looked up Camp Bow Wow. It is a "*premiere doggy Day and overnight camp. A social play all day environment.*" But not everyone can get their dog into Camp Bow Wow. "*All new Camper's must pass a FREE interview and trial day before participating in Day or Overnight Camp.*" You have to schedule an interview. I'm not sure if the owner is interviewed or the pet, I imagine it's both. "*Come sniff us out and see what the bark is all about!*"

I wonder why the pet/car owner put the bumper sticker on the car - is it because he/she was proud to have passed the interview and gotten into this exclusive institution? Or maybe because they perceived that their dog had a great experience at Camp Bow Wow and wants other pets to have the same opportunity? Either way, this is an example of a human trying to interpret how another living thing thinks about something. I think whenever we do that, we (and the other living thing) are at risk of projecting our preferences on the other, something that is really important when we think about empathy between someone who can speak and someone who can't - like animals, babies, and more broadly, groups of people that we want to "help" (immigrants/refugees, poor people, prisoners, people with mental disabilities, etc.)

Before this project, I would have tended to think slightly negatively toward people who appear to prioritize their pets (or animal rights) ahead of people. I think I've changed my mind on this as a result of this project - I don't think there's necessarily something wrong with using your time, treasure, and love primarily for animals - there's no way we can help everyone, we have to make choices and prioritizing animals over people doesn't seem to me to be a misplaced value.

I don't think I'll change my view that dressing up your dog like Leona Helmsley dressed Lucky is somehow disturbing though...

—

I thought the book review of *"Entangled Empathy: An Alternative Ethic for Our Relationships with Animals"* by Lori Gruen introduced some interesting thoughts on the overall topic of

I was particularly struck by the statement: *"What if humanity, with its assurance of moral progress and enlightened rationalism, is the problem?"*

Gruen's main idea, as I understand it, is that a "better" form of empathy is to "define empathy by a vehement attachment to and inhabitation of what we are not: what is not human." She defines empathy beyond its common definition as something similar to sympathy (a one-way feeling) to extend to a two-way interaction: *"a reciprocal infusion of feeling between creatures"*.

—

I listened to an interview with Katy Payne, an acoustical biologist on "On Being" with Krista Tippett. Ms Payne is the first scientist to discover that humpback whales compose ever changing songs to communicate and <u>also</u> that elephants communicate with one another across long distance by infrasound. Can you imagine the same person coming up with both of these discoveries?

A couple interesting observations she made:
• Elephant groups observe periodic moments of absolute quiet and stillness. She it is an awesome experience to see an entire tribe of elephants be still in unison.

- Katy Payne describes how social elephants are - the elaborate greetings members extend each other after just a few hour absence
- she describes observing a grandmother elephant running at top speed to respond to a grandchild's cry across an extended area with numerous elephants present.
- One of the things that supposedly separate ourselves from other animals is that we create and appreciate art. Ms. Perry says that we tend to thing of non-human songs as for the purpose of pro-creation and humans songs as art - in the case of humpback whales, she doesn't see this difference - *"We don't have to have two aesthetics."*

Ms. Perry discusses the sixth extinction, which many scientists believe were are currently in - and our role to help minimize its impact. To preserve wildlife and ecology will require allot of integrated effort of people who are helping with human development, those interested in wildlife conservation. She cautions is not to look towards others as the "bad" people - the "sixth extinction" is a result of *"people who have too much"*. This is our task, she says: *"this is the only planet that we know that has this life - let's not blow it."*

Similar to other conservationists, she believes that there is a vital link between wildlife conservation and taking care of human beings.

I hope this essay encourages you to listen to the podcast. I think you will be joyed to hear this woman's love of life and love for her fellow humans and all living things.

I liked this quote - I think I will put this on the inside of my front door - to remind me every time I leave the house:

> *"If each of us restricts our own lives to what we really need, there'll be more for everyone."*

——-

One topic that comes up sometimes is that question of whether pets go to heaven. Paul VI, said: *"One day we will again see our animals in the eternity of Christ."*

Pope John Paul II said that *"the animals possess a soul and men must love and feel solidarity with our smaller brethren"* and that animals are the *"fruit of the creative action of the Holy Spirit and merit respect"* and are *"as near to God as men are."*

The current Pope, Francis has stated that *"Sacred Scripture teaches us that the fulfillment of this marvelous plan cannot but involve everything that surrounds us and came from the heart and mind of God."*

Now, I myself have no idea if there is an afterlife - I tend think not, at least for individual humans and animals, but it seems clear to me that if there is a heaven, animals would, of course, be welcome. And probably ahead of humans. In fact, perhaps a more appropriate karma would be for animals to go to heaven and humans to return to the earth that is has despoiled.

—

Our twelve year-old cat recently had a medical procedure and now needs to take a pill in the morning and two pills in the evening. For those of you who haven't given a pill to a cat, generally speaking, cats don't like to take pills, or at least mine doesn't. Anyway, I have tried to avoid this task as long as possible - letting my wife and daughter do it. This weekend, they're at the beach and I'm on pill duty. I've now done this twice - last night and this morning and it involves prying open the cat's mouth, shoving the pill down his throat, clamping his mouth shut and squirting water down his throat to try to force him to swallow. My perception is that the cat doesn't know there is a purpose to this procedure - I just have decided to inflict cruelty on him twice a day for no good reason. He runs off afterwards and hides but a few hours later (or the next morning) is back and wants to be petted. I try to explain to him, in words, why I have to do this, but I don't think he understands.

What do I take from this? It reinforces my notion from the Lori Gruen book review that what (may) separate us from animals is the belief in the *"assurance of moral progress and enlightened rationalism"*

that allows to justify immoral practices like slavery, war, inequita-
ble economic systems, and mistreatment of animals in the food
and scientific testing industries.

Round 6: Empathy and the Criminal Justice System

"Prisons do not disappear social problems, they disappear human beings. Homelessness, unemployment, drug addiction, mental illness, and illiteracy are only a few of the problems that disappear from public view when the human beings contending with them are relegated to cages." — **Angela Davis**

The prompt was: Are you ready for round 6? I just finished reading: "*The Master Plan: My Journey from Life in Prison to a Life of Purpose*" by Brett Witter and Chris Wilson and having watched "*When They See Us*" on Netflix and it made me realize how unaware I am of the process that currently incarcerates approximately 2.3 million people in the United States and another 4.6 million on probation or parole. Is the process "fair"? Does it align with our values? Is it something we would be more focused on if it wasn't mostly a "hidden away" issue for many of us who have had very little interaction with the criminal justice system and who have the resources to protect ourselves and our families from most of the negative impacts of incarceration.

Here are a couple of prompts:

• What are your thoughts on whether criminal justice system should be primarily punitive or rehabilitative? Challenge yourself to try to consider the opposite view

- Want to guess at how many people are currently incarcerated due to the inability to make bail? What are your thoughts on the broader question about how money, influence, and social status impacts outcomes in the criminal justice system

- What impact, does our history of race relations impact the criminal justice system. Consider the wording of the thirteenth amendment: *"Neither slavery nor involuntary servitude, except as a punishment for crime whereof the party shall have been duly convicted, shall exist within the United States, or any place subject to their jurisdiction."*

- What thoughts do you have on how to improve our criminal justice system, including how we treat paroled offenders? What prevents us as a country from implementing reforms?

And here are a couple of resources:

- https://www.themarshallproject.org/about

- https://www.themarshallproject.org/tag/life-inside

- https://www.nytimes.com/2018/11/26/opinion/meek-mill-criminal-justice-reform.html

- https://www.yesmagazine.org/issues/is-it-time-to-close-the-prisons/is-it-time-to-close-the-prisons-discussion-guide

———

Responses:

The following is a partial summary of a terrific discussion I had with Dr Gary Lafree, Chair and Professor, Department of Criminology and Criminal Justice over Southside Rye IPAs at Denizens in Silver Spring:

What are your thoughts on whether criminal justice system should be primarily punitive or rehabilitative? Challenge yourself to try to consider the opposite view

While I understand our desire for "vengeance", I very much support a more rehabilitative approach to criminal justice. If we thing of just self-interest, 95% of people incarcerated will eventually be released.. When we walk back to our cars in the dark - do we want to encounter an ex-offender that has been treated in a rehabilitative approach or one who has been treated using a punitive approach? The punitive approach assumes that people don't change. Eleanor and Sheldon Glueck, a husband and wife criminology team did several important studies on criminal rehabilitation. One of their observations was that criminals oftentimes have turning points - new job, getting married, etc. Before World War II, it was often the military - the study would suggest there are ways out of recidivism. If you give up on someone, it's a dead loss for everyone.

Interestingly, the United States is the world leader in prison theory and experimentation. Benjamin Franklin was in involved in an early idea of a penitentiary reform - put the convict in a decent locked cell in solitary confinement with a bible. The Walnut Street jail in Philadelphia has been preserved to document this effort. The experiment failed. The reformers discovered that people in solitary confinement quickly went crazy.

An interesting area of rehabilitative justice is "reintegrative shaming"- pioneered in Australia - which proposes that only when the individual feels remorse can they begin their integration back into society. Reintegrative shaming focuses on a pathway back from the shaming.

One of the interesting things about the US systems of criminal justice is how democratic it is - many other countries don't have juries - we are the jury capital of the world. Additionally, a large number of the participants in the criminal justice system - judges, district attorneys, sheriffs, etc. are elected officials. This makes them much more responsive to the whims of the voters - sometimes a good thing, sometimes a bad thing. Similarly our jury system provides more protection for the accused than the verdict of a judge or tribunal, but also creates a lot more variability in the outcome. It also encourages plea bargaining, which introduces a number of issues as well.

Want to guess at how many people are currently incarcerated due to the inability to make bail? What are your thoughts on the broader question about how money, influence, and social status impacts outcomes in the criminal justice system

The topic of bail is an area that really needs reform - this issue is primarily at the state level, with widely varying rules state by state. The use of middlemen - bail bondsmen, who have relatively few checks on their actions, introduces a profit motive into the issue, further complicating things. In my opinion, bail should be used much more judiciously.

With respect to money, influence, and social status impacting criminal justice outcomes - yes this is a big factor. Would OJ Simpson have gotten off with a public defender? Probably not. I would say, however, that there is good evidence that in many cases, public defenders provide effective counsel for their clients. Again, the public defender process, much like other aspects of the criminal justice system, varies widely State by State. In Texas, for instance, all lawyers have to do public defender cases - a good and bad thing - the defendant with no money is getting the same quality lawyer as the defendant who can pay, but the public defender is more inclined to wrap up the case quicker. Massachusetts is known to have a pretty good public defender program.

What impact, does our history of race relations impact the criminal justice system? Consider the wording of the thir-

teenth amendment: *"Neither slavery nor involuntary servitude, except as a punishment for crime whereof the party shall have been duly convicted, shall exist within the United States, or any place subject to their jurisdiction."*

It has a huge effect - African Americans make up about 12% of the population, but about 50% of inmates. Is this due to racial disparities in criminal enforcement or is it a reflection of actual crime? Victim studies, which are considered to be reliable, indicate that about 50% of violent crimes are committed by African Americans but there is much more nuance to this and there is a self-reenforcing nature to this. There is evidence to support the relationship between enforcement actions such as traffic pullovers, stop and frisk, and parole/probation violations as a cause for crime, or further crime. This is a topic that needs more attention and there are no simple solutions.

What thoughts do you have on how to improve our criminal justice system, including how we treat paroled offenders? What prevents us as a country from implementing reforms?

I offer the following:

1) Continue to build legitimacy for the criminal justice system within communities. This system simply doesn't work without

public support. The criminal justice system is highly dependent on information provided by the public. If/when the public loses faith in the system, the ability to "solve" crimes decreases significantly. There has been some progress in this area - many communities have made big advances toward racially balanced police forces. Civilian review boards have a positive impact. The power to shoot someone is an awesome responsibility and needs lots of review and checks. Body cameras have, and will continue to have a positive impact on police behaviors.

2) In the past several years, with technology, police can tell with a high degree of precision, where guns are being discharged and where crimes are being committed - these are not random occurrences. Use of this technology is, and will increasingly allow the police to deploy their resources more effectively.

3) Reduce the pressure on law enforcement to solve societal problems that result in crime. Most crimes are not reported to the police and most reported crimes are not solved. We put way too much pressure on law enforcement as a response to crime. Law enforcement is reactive after the crime has been committed. For a number of reasons, programs to prevent the causes of crime do not get the same level of public atten-

tion and, as a result, the same level of resources. I am particularly encouraged by the use of Cognitive Behavioral Therapy (CBT, which has shown promising results in cities like Saint Louis and Chicago as a technique for reducing recidivism.)

What holds us back? - we create standoffs by reducing the political discussion to simplicities - an elected or aspiring candidate is either *"tough on crime"* or not sufficiently tough on crime, with less focus on the impact of specific policy ideas. We are also constrained by our inability to discuss issues of race in a careful, nuanced manner. Similarly, discussions of the social impact of large disparities in wealth quickly decompose into accusations of greed vs socialism. Two other topics that have a direct impact on our criminal justice system that we need to have honest dialogue on are guns and police violence.

———

The criminal justice system is a frustrating topic to ponder. Millions of people in jail – more than the populations of many large cities in the United States – the entire population of Chicago. The extent of what I know about the criminal justice system stems from what I've seen on TV, read in the news, and learned in preparation for this assignment. I've only known one individual personally that has spent any significant amount of time in jail – and once they disappeared behind bars, they faded from my life.

How do so many people get locked up? How did they get in that position? Is it fair? Is it just? Some of the answers are obvious. People do bad things and break the law. They ended up in that position because they made poor decisions, they didn't have a choice, or perhaps they were just in the wrong place at the wrong time. Sometimes it's fair. Sometimes just. And many times it's neither.

Is the massive number of incarcerated citizens a result of more bad people committing crimes (and getting caught) or a broken criminal justice system? In my opinion, it's both. Since we're here to discuss the latter, that's where I'll focus my thoughts.

It's clear to me, that some form of imprisonment is required for certain crimes. Murder, rape, and other heinous offenses where there is an immediate need to remove these people from society before they can do more harm makes sense. That's the number one objective in this case. For other crimes that are punishable by jail time it's not as easy to justify the expense nor the value to society in which prison is the punishment – drug offenses, robbery, college admissions scandals? When I think about the criminal justice system, I ponder what is fair, what is just, what are the alternatives, what is the cost, and what value is returned to society? Are we safer because more people are in prison? Nope. Is it tax payer money well spent? Nope. I heard that the cost of operating

Guantanamo Bay was in the ball park of $13 million per prisoner per year. Even at the local and state levels, the average cost nears $45k per year – a respectable salary in a legitimate job, but it's out-of-reach if you've spent time behind bars.

What is the purpose of prison? Is it a proper punishment? An effective deterrent? As a punishment, in many cases, I'm certain the punishment doesn't fit the crime. A life sentence for a cold-blooded killer seems appropriate in the least but other offenses from the ridiculous number of minor drug offenses, legal missteps and white-collar crimes is where the system breaks down for me. You might despise the celebrities that are being sentenced to trivial prison terms for their involvement in college bribing schemes, but I'm not sure that's a fitting punishment. I'd make them pay 10 times or 100 times their bribe and put it directly into scholarships for those that deserve the opportunities. Prison doesn't seem to be an effective deterrent either. If prison was really that bad, wouldn't we have less crime, and therefore fewer people in prison? There's no way I can relate to the real experience of being locked up, but I'm sure it's miserable, depressing, lonely, frightening, and difficult to endure. On the other hand, you have shelter, food, basic necessities and even some limited rights. You might have a job or receive career counseling and other services in preparation for release. For some who have endured homelessness, I wonder if prison is better or worse.

Sadly, the system is self-feeding. It employs thousands of prison guards, administrators, facilities people and extends to prosecutors, judges, and others who make a living in the system. In order to survive, the system needs continuous feeding – new prisoners to sustain and grow the system. No doubt it's broken.

Instead of attaching a certain prison term to varying degrees of offenses, we could consider a more flexible system that allows for retribution based on the type of crime and its impact on society. Murderers and rapists can go straight to jail, but I think that other models may be more effective and more cost efficient in the long run. Put the criminals to work in exchange for a reduced sentence. (I know this does happen but it needs to be done with a much larger population of non-violent offenders.) There is work to be done in our communities, on our infrastructure, and so many other areas where an offender can give back to society in a more positive way vs. eating up space and tax dollars while rotting behind bars. Perpetrators of financial crimes should pay huge fines, work them off until they can, or be given long community service assignments. Jail doesn't seem to create much value for society. Rehabilitation needs to be a huge part of a re-factored system. What's happening today just isn't enough. I'd bet a huge part of the prison population is in desperate need of mental health and drug rehabilitation services. When all of these people serve their time and are released, they need a place to live and a job.

Both are going to be difficult to obtain and can increase the likelihood of returning to prison if those needs go unfulfilled.

I mentioned previously that the system is self-feeding in the pursuit of sustaining and growing the status quo. There are incentives for countless people and governments to keep it alive. But I just don't see the value that is returned to society. What I'd like to see is a criminal justice system designed to eat itself. To shrink – where the goal is to safely and efficiently move people out of the system, stop growing and prevent people from ending up there in the first place. We need more investment in social and health services – especially mental health. More programs that have a positive social impact and reduce the path ways to imprisonment. If it costs $40k+ to house one inmate for a year, imagine what those resources could do to keep people out of the system vs. the non-existent return on taxpayer money when the system is focused on punishment instead of prevention and rehabilitation. Save the jails for the real bad guys and change the punishments to return value to society.

When I consider the potential outcomes of fundamentally changing the system, the economics and value proposition of it all make sense to me, but I'll admit that I could be dead wrong. Perhaps it costs less to house a prisoner than it does to deliver the social services that would keep them out in the first place. There is little incentive for the system to change. It's just hard to fathom that the right thing to do is keep 3 million people tangled in the system. In the long run an investment in alternative methods could have a huge positive impact on society, but what will it take to break the cycle? Can we foster real change that leads us to a better society where people have the opportunities, the education, and the support they need to make good decisions and reduce the numbers of people wasting away their potential as humans rather than being productive members of society? A reduced prison population is a good indicator of a healthy society but we have a long way to go with this complex and frustrating issue.

———

I think that prison should definitely be mostly rehabilitative! Right now in this country for many people (predominantly poor people) I think a prison sentence will effectively destroy their lives. Putting aside questions about whether they are guilty or innocent of whatever crime they are incarcerated for, there are nearly no avenues to a normal life after incarceration. After incarceration, accomplishing any of the things that are needed to get to a stable place becomes very difficult. Gainful employment, new friends/relationships, living decent/safe living accommodations all become significantly more difficult after incarceration. I don't know much about it, but I think the requirements after parole are very intrusive to the point that it makes employment and other things more difficult. With those constraints it makes committing a crime and getting incarcerated again the most likely outcome. I don't see how doing that to people helps society at all.

To remediate these things I think we should make a big distinction between violent crime and non-violent crime. People who are not safe to live free in society should be treated differently than people who have never demonstrated any inclination to harm others. For non-violent offenders we should invest in education, drug treatment, counseling and other programs that will provide them with viable opportunities to succeed in life after incarceration. I think employers who are assured that potential employees don't have a violent past may be more inclined to employ people with a criminal past, especially if they understand that some of the root issues that lead to the initial crime were dealt with during their incarceration. Nothing generates loyalty in an employee like giving people a chance that others might not give them.

In general I think that society has a responsibility to treat everyone with dignity -even people who have made mistakes in life. Again this not something I know much about, but prison is a bad place and I think that right now it only serves to bring out the worst in people. Releasing people back into society after prison, worse than how they started isn't often going to result in anything good happening.

Not directly related to the question, our criminal justice system isn't a fair to poor people. I saw a CBS Sunday Morning article about how destructive posting bail is to many people – often including completely innocent people. Also the fairness of how your trial and sentencing will be is very much dependent on how much you can spend on your defense. Also, having recently watched several of the things about the Central Park 5, you see that prosecution/police are not always as focused on finding the actual criminals for a crime, rather finding someone that they can pin a crime on. Our public servants need to be held accountable for doing their job correctly.

With the Central Park 5 – who were mistreated by the criminal justice system, you can see a lot of what is wrong for those post-paroled. One of the men ended up dealing drugs because he couldn't find work and comply with his parole constraints. He had no means of making an honest living and was forced to a dishonest living. All of the men were emotionally deeply damaged by their time in prison. Also several of them were able to receive an education in prison via a program that has been discontinued.

————

I started my first day of work after graduating from college at Terra Haute Federal Penitentiary. I worked for a public accounting firm that did the financial statement audit of UniCor, the Federal Prison Industry's company that ran the Federal work programs. I spent three weeks in the Terra Haute Penitentiary working in a large room with the accounting staff - all prisoners - convicted of murder, rape, and in one case federal espionage (Art Walker, who sold secrets to the Russians). At the time, I remember being somewhat surprised how friendly and helpful the prisoners were. The guy who sat to my left at the big table I worked with's nickname was "Killer" - I didn't know how to address him otherwise was a devout Christian who read his bible whenever he had downtime. He told me the story of how he had committed murder and how he had the rest of his life to atone for it. Another guy told he that he had gone to prison for killing the man who had raped his ex-wife. His best friend and roommate was convicted of the murder as well because he had used his friend's car to find the man. He told me that his friend had nothing to do with the crime. I don't know if I believe him or not, but it was just something he told me after I got to know him over a couple of weeks.

Kind of a funny story - when Friday came around the first week, I was spending the weekend in Terra Haute - I asked them what there was to do in Terra Haute - I had literally forgotten that they would have no idea what there was to do in Terra Haute - the one guy said - it was about eight years ago that the prison bus had driven through Terra Haute on the way to the prison and he tried to describe the bar/restaurant that he had seen while driving through.

I just recently finished a consulting assignment where I worked with a number of ex-felons in my temporary role as an employment specialist with a local Not-for-profit. It was in this role that I could clearly see that these folks were not at all different from non-felons - except very challenging childhoods, bad breaks, and no assistance when they made mistakes. It was also reinforced on me how hard it is to find a job with a criminal record. This seems to me one of our society's biggest obvious mistakes - we should all be highly incented to work with individuals with criminal records to find employment. Without the ability to work, individuals are highly likely to become re-incarcerated.

———

I spent several hours on the Marshall Project site. There's a wealth of good information there. I wanted to share an extract from a letter from the organization's founder - Neil Barsky, dated 11/15/2014. I think this describes really well how we got to where we are and how fundamentally unfair the Criminal Justice system is:

The seeds of The Marshall Project were planted a few years ago after I read two books. The first, Michelle Alexander's "The New Jim Crow," argues that mass incarceration — which dates roughly from President Ronald Reagan's War on Drugs in the 1980s to the present—represents the third phase of African-American oppression in the United States, after slavery and Jim Crow. Alexander documents how the United States came to be the world's biggest jailer by enacting policies that represented a bipartisan shift in how we address addiction, mental illness, and other non-violent forms of misconduct. Fueled in part by a reaction to civil rights gains and in part by fear of escalating crime, Alexander claims, we enacted tough drug laws, imposed greater mandatory minimum sentences, and ignited a prison boom. Intent can be difficult to prove; impact is irrefutable.

The second, Gilbert King's Pulitzer Prize-winning "Devil in the Grove," explores the case of four African-American males falsely accused of rape in Lake County, Fla., and the vigilante violence that ensued. At the center of the drama was NAACP Legal Defense Fund attorney Thurgood Marshall, the future Supreme Court justice, who bravely but largely futilely fought in Florida's courts to spare these young men's lives. This took place in 1949, before Brown v. Board of Education (a Marshall legal triumph) and before an organized national movement to combat the Jim Crow segregation laws. The national press did not cover the proceedings.

Spurred on by these chapters in American history, I continued to explore our country's system of crime and punishment. What struck me was not only how expensive, ineffective, and racially biased it is, and how difficult it is to find anyone, liberal or conservative, who defends the status quo. But also how our condition has become taken for granted. Other American crises — soaring health-care costs, the failure of public education — typically lead to public debate and legislative action. But the spike in mass incarceration appears to have had the opposite effect: The general public has become inured to the overuse of solitary confinement, the widespread incidence of prison rape and the mixing of teens and adults in hardcore prisons. The more people we put behind bars, it seemed, the more the issue receded from the public consciousness.

———

I'm reading the book "*What a body remembers*" by Karen Stefano, the true story of a woman who survived a sexual assault and later became a lawyer defending people similar to her assailant. She says that: "*I too have fallen in love with my clients... what else can you call it when you know that decades later you will still think about the men and women whose lives you have intersected so briefly with your own? When you wonder if they're still alive, still addicted, still in prison, still funny and smart and wry?*" I believe that if people who are convicted of crimes were not hidden from society in prisons and behind societal barricades, we would feel more compassion and push for rehabilitative responses to crime.

———

I'm going to try to combine two disparate thoughts. The first are some selected lyrics from the song "Crack the Case" by the band Dawes. I think the lyrics might be (re)interpreted as a plea that seeing the other's perspective might be the thing that "cracks the case". The second selected stanza might be applicable to our discussion on people that have legitimately harmed or threatened us and how we might respond if we actually knew them:

I wanna sit with my enemies and say
We should have done this sooner
While I look them in the face
Maybe that would crack the case

It's really hard to hate anyone
When you know what they've lived through
And once they've given you a taste
...Maybe that would crack the case

Findin' out that we occupy
Somebody else's opposin' side
On the banks of some great divide
Two versions of a dream

I wanna call off the cavalry
Declare no winners or losers

And forgive our shared mistakes
You can pick the time and place
Maybe that would crack the case

The second (mostly unrelated) thought is a discussion I heard today on the WAMU (88.5) on the Kojo Naambi show where there was a discussion on DC's currently debated "Second Look" Amendment, which seeks to provide increased opportunities for earlier parole for persons convicted under the age of 18. If you want to learn more or support this initiative, please check out: https://actionnetwork.org/petitions/support-the-second-look-amendment-act

―――

I recently read *"The Master Plan: My Journey from Life in Prison to a Life of Purpose"* by Chris Wilson. I thought this book was amazing. Chris Wilson received a life sentence at age seventeen for murder. Ultimately he was paroled after seventeen years. Shortly after beginning his sentence, Chris Wilson created a plan for his life and sent letters to his sentencing judge every month he was in prison, updating her on his progress against the plan. While in prison, Wilson earned his undergraduate degree, read hundreds of books, and accomplished many other things (read the book to learn more). After being parole, he started several businesses focused on hiring ex-felons and has become a sought-after speaker and motivator. To me, the main message Chris Wilson has is that there is a tremendous amount of inequity, racism, and other areas of unfairness in our society and our criminal justice system but that despite that, each of us is responsible for our lives - felons, families and friends of those incarcerated, prison guards, judges, advocates, and those who choose not to think too much about the overall system.

Chris Wilson mentions Malcolm X several times, which caused me to go back and re-read "Autobiography of Malcolm X". Malcolm X credits prison with giving him the opportunity to become educated: "*I have often reflected upon the new vistas that reading has opened to me. I knew right there in prison that reading had changed forever the course of my life. As I see it today, the ability to read awoke inside me some long dormant craving to be mentally alive.*" I think that this should be a primary focus of the prison system - encouraging and providing opportunities to become educated. With today's technology, it should be possible to offer a prisoner (or anyone else) the opportunity to have the Harvard-level quality education. I have the sense that we are very far from this. I wonder why.

———

Should the Criminal Justice System be primarily punitive or rehabilitative? I would like to add a 3rd purpose: Incarceration in the Criminal Justice System should primarily be to Protect Society. Hannibal Lector should be in jail. But as a general rule, unless the individual is a Danger to Society, I feel they should not be incarcerated. I think the root of most crime is poverty and/or lack of socialization skills or goals for life and/or untreated mental illness. Criminal Justice should focus on fixing those problems and protecting society. Nonviolent crimes should be treated with fines and restrictions.

In most cases, incarceration does not attempt to teach socialization skills or help people develop life goals so it is not rehabilitative. In fact, incarceration can take people who have committed minor crimes or have untreated mental illness and train them to be people who commit major crimes. The Vera Institute of Justice says that "the possibility of rehabilitation is undermined by the brutality and monotony of life behind bars." Of course the purpose of the Criminal Justice System *should* be primarily rehabilitative. But overall, I think it is punitive.

I feel that the actual current end-effect of our Prisons system is purposely punitive as evidenced by such statements as "lock him up and throw away the key. Prisoners are systematically degraded and disrespected, prisons are designed to be ugly, food is designed to be cruddy, the routine is designed to be monotonous, bullying is promoted, extreme loneliness is fostered and mental torture such as solitary confinement are overused. Instead of fostering or teaching people appropriate social behavior, anti-social behavior is promulgated. In "Is There Such a Thing as 'Good' Prison Design?" *Architectural Digest*, 2018 Rachel Slade says that research shows that isolation breeds violence.

In addition to being purposely punitive, mass incarceration is also inadvertently punitive in terms of 1. health, 2. destruction of families and 3. brutality. Incarceration significantly increases a person's risk of acquiring tuberculosis and sexually transmitted infections such as HIV and hepatitis B and C. The risk of these illnesses then spills over to the partners and children of people who have a history of incarceration. Poor prison diet and enforced inactivity cause diabetes, cardiovascular disease and cancer. Mass incarceration represents a major social structure through which racial, class, and gender and health inequalities are produced and maintained in contemporary U.S. society. Unintentionally, incarceration rates represent an important social determinant of a group's health.

Secondly, families are destroyed and children of prisoners are inadvertently punished when they are deprived of their parents while incarcerated. The damage to those children creates another entire generation of people at higher risk of incarceration. The Vera Institute calls it "generational pain." According to Matthew

Larson, a criminal justice professor at Wayne State University, one in nine African-american children has a parent behind bars. This creates a vicious cycle promoting a future generation of anti-social behavior. While this generational pain disproportionally affects children of prisoners, it also affects the elderly. I happened to have a conversation with the sterile supply man for my unit. He shared that he was an only child and that he had been incarcerated. He said that his biggest regret was that being in prison meant that he could not help his elderly mother and that she died alone while he was in jail. He started crying while telling me this. Economically, incarcerated people cannot build credit, buy homes, pay for children's education etc. resulting in enduring poverty which promotes more crime.

Thirdly, the prevalence of violence and sexual assault in US prisons is tantamount to sentencing a person to rape and physical assault for their crime. Although rape and brutal beatings would clearly be considered "cruel and unusual punishment," for some reason, they seem to be an accepted part of the US incarceration experience?

How Many People are currently incarcerated due to the inability to make bail? I had no idea? According to Nicholas Loffredo in "*Unconstitutional to Jail Poor Defendants Who Can't Pay Bail, Feds Argue*" in 2016 the number was 646,000. He described a Georgia defendant,

Maurice Walker, who was initially arrested in the city of Calhoun on a misdemeanor charge of walking while intoxicated. (I did not even know that was illegal?) At the time of the article, Mr. Walker had already spent over 3 months in jail because he could not afford the $160 bail.

Did you see the article this week about Leon Haughton who spent 83 days in jail Maryland for honey? He brought honey from Jamaica but the TSA at BWI thought the honey was methamphetamines and arrested him. He couldn't afford bail and spent 83 days in jail. Tests showed in a couple days that it was honey, not meth. But his trial date was not for 83 days. While he was behind bars, Haughton said he lost his two jobs, his home, his car, his insurance and ruined his credit. *"They messed up my life. I want the world to know that the system is not right. Once I came out, all my insurances collapsed, my credit was destroyed, I lost my jobs, everything was a mess."* Haughton, a father of six, says he now lives in a Maryland hotel as he works to get his life back together. He is terrified to travel. When asked who was responsible for the mistake, the state's office simply said: "There was no error by any agency." Sandra Bland died in jail while her family was trying to scramble together $500 (10% of her bail). Her inability to make bail was equivalent to a death sentence.

The people who can't afford bail are generally the people who can least afford to miss work. Neil once had a client who had spent over a month in jail in PG county on a false identity bench warrant and had not been able to make bail. He literally was not the person for whom the bench warrant was issued. By the time the false identity was discovered, he had lost a really good union job with health insurance +at Washington Gas. His car had been repossessed. He was kicked out of his apartment and was homeless. When Neil tried to sue PG County for false arrest, the case was thrown out because there was no malicious intent. It truly was an accident. The incident truly put this man's life on a downward spiral.

I was happy to see that Alaska and New Jersey have eliminated cash bail and replaced it with Release on Recognizance or House Arrest or electronic monitoring.

How do money, influence and social status impact the criminal justice system? One thing that prevents us from implementing reforms is money. In Iowa they implemented the Public Safety Assessment Program, a pilot which gave judges information on arrested persons that allowed them to estimate whether they were 1. Safe to Release without bail and 2. Likely to return for trial without bail. This had the potential to lower the number of people who needed bail and threatened the livelihoods of Josh and Jacob

Federman, brothers who are the Bail Bondsmen for most of the Midwest. So they donated $74,366.50 to a state senator named Gary Worthan. He put a line item "the public safety assessment pilot program shall be terminated" into the state funding bill that cancelled the Public Safety Assessment Program: https://www.cnn.com/2019/08/30/us/bail-reform-bonds-lobby-ing-invs/index.html The for-profit Prison Industrial Complex has a powerful lobby.

Until I started researching for this essay, I was not aware that even if charges are dropped or you are found completely innocent, you still owe 10% of the bail. With usurious interest. I read about a Mom losing her house because she couldn't pay back the 10% + interest for her innocent son.

What impact does our history of race relations have on the criminal justice system? The 1619 series of articles in the New York Times included a fascinating article by Bryan Stevenson on *"Why American Prisons Owe Their Cruelty to Slavery"*. https://www.nytimes.com/interac-tive/2019/08/14/magazine/prison-industrial-complex-slavery-racism.html?searchResultPosition=2

Bryan Stevenson wrote that: *"The 13th Amendment is credited with ending slavery, but it stopped well short of that: It made an exception for those convicted of crimes. After emancipation, black people, once seen as less than fully human "slaves," were now seen as less than fully human "criminals."*

The provisional governor of South Carolina declared in 1865 that they had to be "restrained from theft, idleness, vagrancy and crime." Laws governing slavery were replaced with Black Codes governing free black people — making the criminal-justice system central to new strategies of racial control." Basically, people of color are "presumed" to have inherently criminal natures.

According to Bryan Stevenson, although problems with the system stretch farther back, the "prison-industrial complex" started in the '80s, with the War On Drugs. Between 1980 and 1984, FBI anti-drug funding went from $8 million to $95 million. At the same time, funding for drug treatment and prevention was, illogically, drastically cut. By increasing penalties for "crack" cocaine but not for "powder" cocaine, inner-city, communities of color were targeted. African Americans were sent to jail at alarming rates for nonviolent crimes. Fast-forward a few decades…we have mass incarceration. The US sends vastly more people to prison than any other nation on Earth, and people of color make up most of the US incarcerated population. The US has 4% of the world's population and 26% of the world's incarcerated people. In 1970, US prisoners numbered fewer 300,000; since then, that number has grown to 2.2 million incarcerated. Plus another 4.5 million on probation or parole. Because of three strikes laws and mandatory sentences, "broken windows policing" people are sentenced to life without parole for stealing a bike or possession of marijuana. Central to understanding this practice of mass incarceration and excessive punishment is the legacy of slavery. Bryan Stevenson wrote that *"The 13th Amendment is credited with ending slavery, but it stopped well short of that: It made an exception for those convicted of crimes. After emancipation, black people, once seen as less than fully human "slaves," were now seen as less than fully human "criminals." The provisional governor of South Carolina declared in 1865 that they had to be "restrained from theft, idleness, vagrancy and crime." Laws governing slavery were replaced with Black Codes governing free black people — making the criminal-justice system central to new strategies of racial control."* Basically, people of color are "presumed" to have inherently criminal natures.

"Neither slavery nor involuntary servitude, except as a punishment for crime whereof the party shall have been duly convicted, shall exist within the United States, or any place subject to their jurisdiction."

How to improve our criminal justice system. Change the focus from Making Money for the private prison industry to Protecting Society and Rehabilitation. The Vera Institute of Justice issued a report called *"Reimagining the Prison"* https://www.vera.org/reimagining-prison

They visited the German correctional system where prison is called *Sozialtherapeutische Haftanstalten* (social therapy institute where prisoners live in small social groups with pets and are treated with dignity) and devised a system called T.R.U.E., an acronym:

- Truthfulness (to oneself and others),

- Respectfulness (toward the community),

- Understanding (ourselves and what brought us here), and

- Elevating (into success)

 They propose changing the current basis of the prison system from:

- Retribution. A theory of justice in which the purpose of criminal penalties is to punish individuals for crimes committed. Retributive models are retroactive in nature: they punish what has already occurred and contemplate no effect on future behavior.
- Incapacitation. A theory of crime prevention in which prison's purpose is to separate people from society and thereby limit their ability to commit additional crimes.
- Deterrence. A theory of crime prevention that posits that by seeing punishment enacted on others—or by experiencing punishment them.

Vera proposes *"that <u>Human Dignity be the foundational, organizing principle of the nation's corrections system</u>. This principle recognizes every person's intrinsic worth and capacity for self-control, autonomy, and rationality."*

In practice, this theory converts to 3 principles:

Principle 1: Respect the intrinsic worth of each human being as manifested by requiring staff to call prisoners by their names, not numbers. Prisoners wear clothes of their individual choosing, not uniforms and by providing high quality, respectful, prompt healthcare etc.

Principle 2: Elevate and support personal relationships; as manifested by promoting interaction with people outside prison and housing groups of 10-15 prisoners to live together. Each group is supported by social workers and psychologists. The goal of these sections is to give the prisoners a chance to refurbish socialization deficits. Prison design ensure that prison relationships are facilitated in the layout of the prison itself-private & meeting rooms, open spaces, kitchens to cook together, no overcrowding, pets, well lit, access to nature etc.

Principle 3: Respect a person's capacity to grow and change as manifested by recognizing that no matter what behavior may have landed a person in prison, they still have the potential to change. Prisons should provide suitable opportunities for all incarcerated people to pursue productive activities and to grow and develop as people. Such as up to date reading materials and education opportunities, mental health counseling, addiction treatment, work opportunities with fair pay, the right to vote, case managers who jointly develop goals and plans to achieve these goals with prisoners, promoting opportunities for prisoners to positively impact their families etc.

What prevents us as a country from implementing reforms? As stated previously, one thing that prevents us from implementing reforms is the money the Prison Industrial Complex makes and the political influence that same money buys. UNICOR also known as Federal Prison Industries, on its own website https://www.bop.gov/inmates/custody_and_care/unicor_about.jsp , while boasting that *"Its mission is to prepare inmates for successful reentry through job training"* and claiming that participation in prison work reduces recidivism by 24%, also brags that average pay is 23 cents-$1.15. It states that "In FY 2017, UNICOR had $483.8 million in profit" and that "FPI's derives over 50% of its sales from the Department of Defense." It seems like if their mission truly was to help prisoners, they could pay them minimum wage and give this money to them upon release so that they would have some money to live off while they are looking for a job. After his release, it took Chris Wilson 52 days to find a job. And he says that is unusually quick. His $100 per month parole fee was waived but most parolees have to pay that plus $40 twice a week for drug screens. Chris Wilson wrote that he knew people in Baltimore who sold drugs to pay their parole expenses.

Another fact is that the absence of mental health programs means that prisons are the primary source of mental health care in the US. (pretty universally, atrocious health care) We incarcerate our mentally ill instead of treating them. Until we have functioning universal mental health care in the US, the prisons is where we will house our mentally ill. People call the police on schizophrenic people and they end up in prison. A nurse I know who moonlights at Holy Cross's Germantown facility told me that last weekend a person climbed onto a roof naked because they believed that evil currents were being sent to a roof and they wanted to block the currents. After a 24 hour suicide watch (they weren't suicidal), they were jailed for indecent exposure and trespass.

I won't even start to discuss how paying such low wages depresses wages for people outside of jail trying to get fair pay for their work. Electronic Services are listed as one of the labors FPI provides. If you can pay a prisoner 23 cents/hour to do your kitting, potting and soldering, why on earth would you pay a free person $15 to do the same work? In 2017 Unicor had prisoners sew $100 million dollars worth of military uniforms. Crushing small businesses who just can't compete because they have to pay a minimum wage to their workers. They falsely call this injustice "a jobs training program," but it's clear that the prison-industrial complex is more concerned with profiting from the labor of these human beings then they are in rehabilitation

Round 7: Empathy and Immigration

Here were the prompts for our penultimate round:

- How has your own family's immigration story that have helped shape your views on immigration?
- How does your belief system (religious or not) inform your views on immigration?
- Are there any personal experiences (interactions with immigrants) that have impacted your views on this topic?
- What obligation do we have to "take in"/"take care" of immigrants (general question)
- What obligation do we have to "take in"/"take care" of immigrants that have migrated due to actions we as a country have caused?
- What are your general thoughts on "legal" vs "illegal" immigration?
- Imagine yourself in the "shoes" of an immigrant fleeing extreme hardship or danger - would your thoughts on legal vs illegal immigration be different?

Responses:

One of the most fruitful effects of this project is that I have become interested in and pursued information on topics that I previously virtually ignored because I knew so little about them. An example of this is the subject of incarceration and the US criminal justice system. After reading The Master Plan I am now reading The New Jim Crow (I highly recommend it) and am becoming convinced that our current system is unjust, discriminatory and, yes, the new Jim Crow. After becoming more interested in this subject, I use it as one way of viewing presidential candidates, e.g., I don't support Kamala Harris because she declined to endorse ballot initiatives that would have reformed the three-strikes law and ended the death penalty. She even appealed a federal court decision striking down the death penalty as unconstitutional. I mention my new interest in the criminal justice system during our round on immigration as a caveat that I really am a novice on the subject of immigration. But, as I start reading up on it, I hope to develop a sustained interest and involvement. That being said, here are a few of my preliminary thoughts. I truly believe that the future of our planet depends on going in the direction of a world community. I am a globalist, not a nationalist or what Trump calls a "patriot". Our country needs diversity in order to thrive. We need to welcome "the tired, the poor, the huddled masses yearning to breathe free" and commit to integrating newcomers into our society. Tearing children from their parents is an abomination and clearly should not be done. But . . . it's complicated. Warmly welcoming all who want to come to the US is naive. Low-skilled native-born Americans rightly resent immigrants who compete with them for low-paying jobs. People are challenged when asked to live in close proximity with others who are culturally different and this challenge must be addressed. Admiral Stavridis (formerly Supreme Allied Commander for NATO) has pointed out that the Trump Administration has called up over 2000 military troops to support the approximately 5000 already on duty at the border. This number dwarfs the number of military in Syria and approaches the number in Afghanistan. He decries the use of military as a front line "defense" against immigrants and advocates for interagency cooperation to deal humanely with migrants crossing the border. He also advocates for international cooperation involving Mexico and the nations of Central America.

Some statistics stand out and startle (just as certain photographs do). At least 23,000 people have died or gone missing since 2011 trying to cross bodies of water in search of safe haven. Think of the impact on their loved ones, not knowing whether they are dead or alive. And I am appalled at the absurd notion of building a "huuuge" wall to deter desperate immigrants. Not only does it cost money that should be well spent elsewhere, but it is ugly, ineffective and damages wildlife trails . . . as well as being an archaic throwback to the olden days.

The story of my Grandparents fleeing the Saarland because they were "status quo-ers" made a big impression on me as a child. Being questioned in the train by Nazis and quickly coming up with the excuse that they were going to a sporting event, not fleeing seemed dangerous and exciting to me. After finally escaping, the idea that the US might not take them would seem preposterous.

As a kid, it seemed like Grandma's family had been in the US so long that their story seemed more boring.

With respect to what my religion and value system tell me is that that it is absolutely clear that the Judeo-Christian response to immigrants fleeing danger should be welcoming.

- *"Do not forget to show hospitality to strangers, for by so doing some people have shown hospitality to angels without knowing it."* (Hebrews 13.2)

- *"If any of your fellow Israelites become poor and are unable to support themselves among you, help them as you would a foreigner and stranger, so they can continue to live among you. Do not take interest or any profit from them, but fear your God, so that they may continue to live among you. You must not lend them money at interest or sell them food at a profit. 38 I am the LORD your God, who brought you out of Egypt to give you the land of Canaan and to be your God."* (Leviticus 25.35-38)

- *"Do not mistreat or oppress a foreigner, for you were foreigners in Egypt."* (Exodus 22:21)

- *"'When a foreigner resides among you in your land, do not mistreat them. 34The foreigner residing among you must be treated as your native-born. Love them as yourself, for you were foreigners in Egypt. I am the LORD your God."* (Leviticus 19:33-34

- *"For I was hungry and you gave me something to eat, I was thirsty and you gave me something to drink, I was a stranger and you invited me in"* (Matthew 25:35)

With respect to personal experiences that have helped shape my views on this topic, nursing is one of the occupations that gets you a H-1C visa. My current unit is more than have immigrant nurses on these H-1C visas. Primarily from Africa along with a few from India and the Philippines. And the spouses and unmarried children under 21 years of age of nurses are entitled to H-4 classification so they can come to the US as well.

One ethical issue with this is the fact that this H-1C visa is taking trained nurses from countries who are in desperately need of their services.

———

All four of my grandparents immigrated in their early 20s from southern and central Italy in the first decade of the 20th century as many of the immigration laws we have now we're in the process of being debated and legislated. Until then, the only immigration laws were those passed following the Gold Rush and during the building of the railroads. Those laws (known as the Chinese Exclusion Acts) targeted Chinese who had immigrated in great numbers to work the goldfields and help build the tracks. I recall listening to my paternal grandfather, for whom I am named, tell stories of the trip across the Atlantic in steerage, cramped with hundreds of others and kept optimistic in an otherwise trying journey with the promise of the opportunity that they had been told was America. Absent other legislation, they were still required to be deposited on Ellis Island where their documents were examined and their health checked. My grandfather was kept in quarantine for several days because of a cough, was examined daily by someone and finally released, whereupon he settled in lower Manhattan. Both he and my maternal grandmother (my other grandparents died before I was born) were required to register annually by visiting a local immigration office as aliens, to renew their ability to remain in the US. During those visits, they had to provide evidence of working and the ability to support themselves. My grandfather was a journeyman carpenter and my grandmother a garment worker. Remember, those were the days before federal welfare programs. I was left with the impression that they had to be self-reliant in order to remain and that concept has colored my thinking to this day. Our ability to have developed into a global power so soon after our Civil War, to have saved the world from the evils of Nazism and Fascism, and to have dominated the twentieth century with innovation that accelerated the standard of living in many allied countries, was largely the result of the contributions of immigrants. I believe we remain a nation of immigrants, legal immigrants who contributed to the rich heritage we have enjoyed.

My basic beliefs involve the notion that we are a nation of laws that must be obeyed and enforced in order to manage the diverse ethnicities of immigrants into an assimilated culture. Legal immigration is a desirable mechanism to bring the diversity of other cultures of the world into America, continuing that which brought my grandparents here. Religion is a factor only as it may relate to the inability of immigrants to assimilate or lawfully participate in our society while practicing their faiths. The protection of religion in our constitution allows such practice and our tolerance for a wide variety of religions has con tribute to the assimilation of those so devoted. If the motivation of an immigrant is to come to my country, participate positively in its opportunity and rewards, it is their responsibility to assimilate to us, rather than the other way around. That does involve reasonable efforts of citizen groups to assist in that assimilation; ESL is a perfect example thereof.

Are there any personal experiences (interactions with immigrants) that have impacted your views on this topic? Yes. Several co-workers have been immigrants who have studied to be naturalized. During our several relationships, we engaged each other in discussion of historical events or cultural issues to help them understand what they were required to learn…although I was a very accomplished baseball player, I failed miserably trying to explain the game in a way they could understand. In a couple of cases, I was invited to their naturalization celebration with their families and was honored to do so.

What obligation do we have to "take in"/"take care" of immigrants? As indicated above, if we wish the assimilation to be as uneventful and positive as possible, we should extend ourselves to legal immigrants short of providing income and benefits. Their presence represents respect for the laws under which they arrived and wish to remain. One only needs to experience their naturalization day to feel the reward for extending ourselves on their behalf. I have traveled overseas to countries whose residents could not be more helpful in providing directions to places or recommendations to places of interest. I have also been the recipient of gross indifference, bordering on rudeness, simply because I am American. Putting ourselves in the immigrant's shoes will guide us but all immigrants should be aware of their responsibility to have a mean of support in place before they embark.

What obligation do we have to "take in"/"take care" of immigrants that have migrated due to actions we as a country have caused? This is a politically-charged issue at the very least. Accordingly, the definition of "actions we...caused" will be colored with the politics of the person defining it. My suspicion of politicians and their political agenda on this issue prevents me from believing what they are telling us. Since we have immigration laws that include desired handling of those migrants, they should be the prescription for their care and management. If the laws require change, there should be reasonable debate for the change thereof but not simply because the problem has been exacerbated by the lack of enforcement or political expediency. The reason for their immigration is a secondary consideration to the established processes and requirements by which we have accepted immigrants.

What are your general thoughts on "legal" vs "illegal" immigration? If you are immigrating legally, we will assist you as a nation. If you are here illegally, you are absorbing resources away from citizens. In my view, extenuating circumstances such as the families that have grown over years of illegal residence are issues that are secondary and of no input to the enforcement of the laws. By entering illegally, those folks put themselves in jeopardy and there are consequences for those actions that are unpleasant at best. To this end, if those illegal immigrants have been here for so many years, they could have demonstrated their intent by initiating the legal process of naturalization as did so many others. The passage of time is no remedy to the illegal entry that precipitated the circumstance. That is perceived by many as rigid, but the need for law enforcement regarding resident entry is a cardinal issue to preservation of the republic.

Imagine yourself in the "shoes" of an immigrant fleeing extreme hardship or danger - would your thoughts on legal vs. illegal immigration be different? Asylum is well-documented in the existing immigration laws and provides a manageable process by which to apply for, receive and maintain asylum status en route to citizenship. There must be a credible process by which to legitimize asylum seekers from those who would otherwise be of questionable character or health that should not be permitted to enter. America has been a sanctuary for asylum-seekers for centuries but the recent events indicate clearly that this qualification is being prostituted for political purposes that have negative consequences for the country. I am the offspring of legal immigrants who were afforded nothing but an opportunity to assimilate by being productive and self-reliant. They did so within the laws and our family has thrived as a result. While I have searched extensively, I have failed to uncover persuasive discussion that justifies the current handling of those who would enter because of extreme hardship or danger, or the relaxation or abandonment of existing laws to accommodate the en masse asylum applications. While I cannot correctly envision being in the shoes of a fleeing immigrant, neither can anyone else, and I am certain their fear and apprehension at an uncertain future is all-consuming. While I may be somewhat sympathetic, the overriding concern is the prostitution of our political and financial well-being as a nation that results from the lack of enforcement of existing laws. With an illegal population in excess of 10 million, according to several sources, the current abandonment of existing laws by which to manage immigration is not an appropriate solution and only serves to propel the political agenda of those whose sole objective is the exploitation of those involved for their political gain rather than for the benefit of the immigrants themselves.

———

Belief in a God demands that we care for those who are fleeing oppression in their own lands. The world was created by God who meant for the earth to be shared by all and be everyone's home. Nations since the beginning of time have erred by not giving all people the rights granted by God. It is all of our responsibilities to try and grant that right.

In the Bible the book of Genesis chapter 1, verse 26 says that God created all things: "*cattle.........seed bearing plants, fruits, etc. and Man... whom God made in His own image and likeness*". God saw His creation as good. God continued to say that mankind had dominion over this creation. If we believe this mandate from God then we must do everything we can to take care of this creation. That means giving mankind a suitable place to live. When conditions in a nation are such that mankind can't live under tyranny or oppression, then it is mankind's responsibility to help man go to places where he can live in harmony with God's command of taking care of his creation. A second story in the Bible relates how God helped the Israelites who were in enslaved in Egypt return to their own land where they could live as they wanted. God not only helped them by parting the Red Sea so that they could cross to freedom, but also provided food, Manna, for their sustenance. Immigration to countries where man can carry out God's will is a right given by God. We must follow this command.

My parents immigrated to the United States in 1937 just prior to World War II from Nazi Germany. My father, a professor was told that his political views would prevent him from ever teaching in Germany. My mother, a Social Worker, was reported to the Gestapo as being politically unstable and unemployable. My uncle, a Roman Catholic Priest, was warned by his Bishop that his life was in jeopardy if he did not leave Germany. Another uncle sold his store in a very small town in Germany and fled to a large city to vanish among the crowds. The United States of America was a haven for my parents and uncle. Our lives have been enriched and blessed for over 80 years because of the immigration laws in the United States.

After the war was over, our family went to visit relatives in Germany several times. We were on a steamboat and left from New York City. As the boat was pulling out of New York harbor we passed the Statue of Liberty. She was the loveliest Lady I could imagine as a young 10 year old girl. Each time I have sailed out of New York I stood in awe of her upraised lit torch-bearing-arm to welcome those seeking refuge and freedom.. I have toured Ellis Island and have seen Immigration Responses the places where hundreds of thousands of immigrants came to leave oppression and seek the freedom that the United States has given so many people in this country. This refuge must never disappear from the United States of America! It is what America is – a land of refuge for many!

———

I came across Maeve Higgins July 19, 2019 New York Times Essay: "Upset by the Scenes on the Border? Look Closer To Home". Maeve Higgins is an Irish-born immigrant, comedian, and author/essayist. In her essay, she describes spending a day in immigration court in lower Manhattan. I think the essay is really good - it combines information I didn't know with insightful descriptions of the people she observes in the courtroom.

Some of the things I learned include:

- There are currently about 900,000 people waiting for their immigration court cases. This number is about 50% higher than when our current president took office. Less than 5% of these are due to criminal convictions.

- Unlike other courts, immigration courts do not provide legal counsel if you can't afford it - only about 14% of detained immigrants are able to obtain legal counsel.

- Also, unlike other courts, the immigration court system does not fall within the judicial branch - it is administered by the Executive Branch's Justice Department.

Maeve Higgins' description of guard who shouts at people to move who are trying to find out where to in the lobby of the immigration court, shackled defendants trying to articulate themselves to the judge, children observing their shackled parents trying to understand what is happening, sympathetic judges who take time to explain what happens next and other judges who "treat immigrants like parts on an assembly line" force the reader to vicariously participate in what is happening.

Maeve Higgins' finishes the essay describing how "hidden" immigration court is from the neighborhood - you have to go inside to become aware of what is happening. I really liked her closing sentence:

"To conserve our souls, immigration court is a spectacle we must choose to look at."

——

Years ago, I worked with a woman who escaped from Vietnam in her early teens with her family. Her family's first attempt was by boat, which was confiscated along with most of her family's wealth (gold hidden in the boat). Their second and successful attempt was in another boat along with a number of other emigres. She and her family spend almost a year in a refugee resettlement island with no access education. Upon arrival to the US, she started 9th grade in the Fairfax public school system not knowing a word of English. By the end of the first semester she knew English. She graduated high school in four years, graduated from George Mason four years later and has worked in the field of government contracting compliance ever since, providing financial support to her parents and sibling. I have never met someone with the combination of work ethic, devotion to family, fierce determination for her children's success, and belief that her success is the result of her efforts as well as the efforts of her parents and others.

To me, her story is an example of how our country benefits by welcoming immigrants who are willing to face incredible obstacles to get here and succeed here - I believe it truly is the "secret sauce" of our Country's economic success and the key to our continued success.

———

Immigration is a challenging topic for me. I think that part of the reason is that I really don't spend much time thinking about it. I certainly don't feel much of a connection to it. I was born here in the US, and I'm not well connected to my family's "immigration story." For many of us that qualify as Gen-X, we may be up to two generations removed from that story. Sure, we can have DNA testing done to fill in the gaps, and our parents or grandparents can share their parts of the story, but we'll never live it. We'll never understand it. And we may find it difficult to empathize with it, after all, we are already here.

For those of us living in America, there's nearly a zero percent chance we would be faced with a situation that would cause us to migrate somewhere outside this country. So, yes, it's difficult for me to really understand, and thus, I have difficulty forming strong opinions about the matter. I'm not blind to the perspectives – I see the polarization in the media, and I agree with both ends of the spectrum. Yes, we should show compassion and take in everyone who is suffering and left with migration as their only option to survive. Yes, we should have controlled immigration for the sake of the people that live here and those that wish to join us. Open doors – yes. Closed borders – yes. I think that it's the black and white nature of the issue that contributes to the problem. We're between a rock and a hard place. Nothing gets accomplished in an effective and positive way. It's a complex issue.

My faith leads me to pursue empathic actions, but I am reminded that "empathy is not a uniformly positive attribute." (https://cis.org/Wahala/Blinded-Empathy). In other words, our "empathy" is often misguided. There are consequences to our actions – even with the best intent. If immigrants keep coming here for better jobs, what will happen when we reach a point when there are no more jobs? Maybe that's some sort of natural equilibrium that would occur when the opportunities that bring people hear are gone. Supply and demand. Can we make the argument that we should open the floodgates until we reach that point? I don't know if we want to find out. A world in which those opportunities don't exist wouldn't likely be good for anyone – immigrants and natural born citizens alike.

We need to shift the debate away from "let them in" vs. "keep them out" or, if they are already here, "let them stay" vs. "kick them out." The issue to far too complex and nuanced for how it is handled by our politicians and portrayed in the media. We need to look at root causes. Why do people want or need to migrate?

Those are the problems we need to solve. If we didn't have wars, people going hungry, religious persecution or if we had more jobs, stable economies and fair governments in countries that are sources of migrants we'd have less forced/no-choice immigration. I'd love to see migration become a choice based on the weather and not survival.

———

It looks to me that the world has more migrants than ever. Millions of people had and have no option but to leave their homes due to wars and other situations. My focus will be more on the Central American and Mexican immigrants' plight. I'm sure you all know that folks from El Salvador, Guatemala, Honduras , etc. have virtually no options if they don't want to join the local gang. If one doesn't join they can be killed. If one does, they will have to commit acts of violence including murder. One young man from (I think) Honduras tried to leave his village and migrate up north. He was caught and sent back. When his local gang caught up with him, they beat him severely and threw acid on his face. He tried two more times, and two more times he got sent back. On his last return, he was killed by the gang.

On top of that the economic hardship faced by these Paisanos (countrymen) is immense. I have an American friend who lives in

Mexico and comes here to work at times. He told me that in Mexico for a full day's work with concrete and rebar he would be lucky to make ten dollars. It's no wonder why people want to come here and make a better life.

We absolutely have an obligation to take in immigrants. We are perhaps the richest country on earth and have so much. When so much of the world is suffering as a result of criminal governance by "world leaders" it seems flat out wrong not to help them. Sadly, many Americans think immigrants are here to take something away from them, or milk the system. The rhetoric being spewed by our demagogue despotic president has made everything worse on this front. Many people buy into this xenophobic lie. The fact of the matter is that America is made of immigrants. Native Americans are really the only true natives to this land. Diversity has made this country great, not homogeneity. Similarly, plants are healthy when not planted in a monoculture. Companion planting benefits all involved.

My personal experience with immigrants is daily. My friend and helper at work (let's call him Juan Doe) is from Durango, Mexico. His mother and father live on their ranch where they have a nice house and many fruit trees and other crops like peanuts. His two brothers are also here. His two sons and daughter were born here and are citizens. He usually works seven days a week like all the

Mexicans I know. The stereotype image of a guy napping under a saguaro is false. Mexicans are the opposite of lazy and have the best attitude toward work. One that I have tried to adopt. I see it as work is life and let's enjoy it. These guys play music, and eat lunch promptly at 12:00 often bringing hot plates and comals (skillet) and cook up great food on site. Then they work again.

We are landscapers, specializing in irrigation systems, so we go house to house on service calls. At every job site, if the owner has any projects or work being done, 95% of the workers are Mexican or Central American. I am a gevacho (white guy, nicer than gringo which is like an outsider) and when Juan and I pull up to a job site it often happens that the workers look very serious or scared. They see a gevacho and a mexicano together, and maybe think I am some kind of jefe (boss). At one job the workers were all sitting around the comal, and when we arrived everyone hopped to it and started to look busy. When we say hello to them in Spanish, the serious looks and fear go away. Speaking someone's language I feel is invaluable and one of the best ways to erode divisions.

The fear is real. My friend Juan has been deported before. To sneak back into the Estdos Unidos, one hires a coyote (person who smuggles people across the border). It cost him $7000.00, and he rode in a car trunk with another man and elderly woman. My friends tell me when there has been an ICE raid too. There is a Mexican supermarket here called "Paisanos". Couple of years ago, ICE rounded up 35 men, women, and children. Also there are raids on the restaurants and hotels downtown. Once while driving between jobs I was behind a heavy duty looking law enforcement vehicle. My friend Juan was palpable worried and asked me to drive further away from it. One thing that really taught me something about the fear is when I recounted the Paisano's raid to a different immigrant friend. His expression changed and I felt like I had upset him. Perhaps I should have kept my mouth shut.

Immigrants are good people and hard workers, who only want to improve their situation like any of us. They flee horrific situations and the cartel runs things. The latest violence in Culiacan, Mexico bears witness to this. The Mexican government tried to capture Joaquin Guzman's (El Chapo) son in a raid. The cartel rolled in and started killing police, soldiers, and civilians. They had a 50 caliber machine gun mounted to a heavy truck. In one video I saw, posted by cartel members on the way to this massacre, showed the view from inside their SUV with their heavy weapons including a rocket propelled grenade launcher. Music was playing on the radio. Outgunned, and blood covering the streets, the Mexican president called off the raid not wanting more loss of life.

I can't get into all of the vastly complicated geopolitical situations all over the world causing so much migration. But when I look at the problem, I think the solution is to work with other countries to improve conditions and create some opportunity in the countries people are fleeing. But this would involve the United States taking a very different tone than currently, and also beginning to rebuild our reputation of being a leader and example to the world. This is not going to happen with this criminal administration, that can't even tell the truth.

As each of us is just one person, we can only do what we can do. Personally, I try to show some sort of solidarity with my paisano friends. This year I started listening to Mexican and Colombian music almost exclusively. This came about by listening to the Mexican radio station with Juan. I'd hear a tune I liked and download it. Now I have hours of Cumbias on my ipod. Also listening to the advertisements helped me improve my Spanish, and are quite amusing. For example "nadie have un spicy chicken sandwich como Wendy's", the American product is in perfect English within a perfect Spanish sentence. This station also plays ads explaining to immigrants that they have rights and don't have to open the door to ICE unless they have a warrant. Also many ads for abrogados (lawyers) specializing in immigration issues.

I also think food is a great way to connect with people. Mexican food is awesome! Do you know anyone who doesn't like tacos?

Perhaps it is easier for me to show solidarity with immigrants because of where I live. There is ample opportunity to here. One woman at my favorite taco shop, and a man at the beer store, found out I speak Spanish, and now they speak Spanish only to me. Somehow it feels like an honor.

My advise? Eat tacos and listen to cumbia. Sonia, en Espanol!

—-

I've listened to several episodes of the podcast "Only in America with Ali Noorani", which I think is really insightful. In the episode: "Bearing Witness Along the Border", Ali interviews Beth Cossin, the site director for the Esperanza Legal Assistance Center. She talked about a recent trip she made to Ciudad Juarez to visit a church that ICE releases boarder crossers that they have apprehended. I like the comment she made about the importance of telling the stories of the immigrants:

"In America, we do a great job of insulating ourselves from the uncomfortable things that we just don't want to deal with and so it's important for us to venture out and to actually bear witness to the reality of suffering, to the reality of crisis, to the reality of tragedy, and then to bring that back to the spaces we occupy and disturb the norm and to call ourselves into a new awakening."

At the end of each episode, Ali Norani, asks each guest to complete the sentence: "Only in America….". Here was her answer, which I think challenges us to meet the promise of the inscription on the Statue of Liberty and what I think is the promise and the great strength of our country - welcome and embrace of refugees. *"Only in America do we have the opportunity to actually be the beautiful nation that migrants and refugees sacrifice everything to get to. We can do better than we are doing right now."*

I read "Enrique's Journey" by Sonia Nazario. It is the story of a 14 year-old Honduran boy's attempt to find his mother in North Carolina. He succeeds on his eight attempt after suffering a vicious beating by MS 13 gang members in Mexico. I think the book is excellent in putting the reader "in the shoes" of someone trying to illegally enter this country. The book includes a lot of background information on the causes and impacts of migrations in the Americas. One cause is political instability in several Central American countries as a result of U.S. active and covert actions in our cold war with communism. Another one is the exporting of MS13 gang members that formed in Los Angeles to El Salvador, many of whom had little connection by that point to their home country. Another major cause of the political instability in Central America are the drug cartels that have developed to feed U.S. citizens demand for illegal drugs. Global warming is increasingly impacting Central American agriculture. According to

US AID, Honduras is one of the places most vulnerable to climate change, despite almost no contribution to the problem.

Do we have a responsibility to help a situation that we have helped create? I definitely think so. But what should we do?

In Sonia Nazario's afterward is a nuanced assessment of the pros and cons of immigration, and in particular, illegal immigration. The author effectively articulates the negative impacts of illegal immigration on the immigrants themselves, strain on our social safety nets, and particularly in states with high numbers of illegal immigrants: "*a decline of many public public services, namely schools, hospitals, and state jails and prisons. Classrooms are overcrowded. Hospital emergency rooms have been forced to closed...*". Sonia Nazario describes U.S. immigration policies as "schizophrenic" - reflecting U.S. businesses need for cheap laborers versus a hardening of U.S. citizens views on illegal immigrants.

The author says that immigration experts have concluded that the only effective strategy is improvement in the economies of "immigrant-sending" countries. She points to family size in poor Central American countries as one of the most important causes of the poverty that contributes to illegal immigration and describes the success of Mexico's family planning campaign to reduce the number of children per family from 6.8 in 1970 to 2.2 in 2012.

In March of this year, however, our current president announced he would cut aid appropriated by Congress to Central American countries because they have failed to stop migration flows. In June, over $550 million in aid was withheld.

I liked the following quote from Richard Holwill, deputy assistant secretary of state for inter-inter-americas affairs in the 1980s about the cuts in aid to Central America: "*National security rests on economics as well as anything. We can't just pull up a drawbridge, wall out the rest of the world and say, hey, we can survive here in this island that we call the United States. We are interconnected, and our security is enhanced by ensuring that their world is stable.*"

If you get a chance – I encourage you to read "Enrique's Journey" or go to www.enriquesjourney.com to see pictures of Enrique and his family.

Round 8: Learning By Teaching

"There's a tangible benefit to us when we give other people advice in arena where we hope to improve"

It turns out that spending the last ten months trying to learn more about empathy in connection with some of the most challenging problems of our humanity - racism, immigration, our treatment of animals, our stewardship of our environment - is really hard and sometimes unpleasant. I've been struggling to think about how to wrap up a topic that I feel we have barely scratched the surface of - and sometimes when we have scratched, have found things we don't want to see.

I explained the challenge to my daughter and she suggested that I consider the "Advice Giving Effect" as a way of surmounting problems that we may not be able to solve ourselves. It turns out that the action of giving advice to others can have an amazing effect of providing clarity to ourselves.

So... I ask you to provide advice to someone who asks your advice on how to live a good life:

- what do we (collectively) need to do to move in the right direction?
- what role does empathy have in the direction we should take?

- what are you (the advice giver) doing now or going forward to help us move in the right direction?
- what recommendation do you have to the advice seeker about how to help us collectively move in the right direction?

The first part of this chapter includes the interviews participants did of people they thought modeled compassionate empathy. The second part includes participants responses to the above question.

Interviews

Cathy is an Incredible Human. She is a Recreation Therapist at NIH. Every day at 11am, she comes and talks to an exceptionally difficult multi-drug resistant TB patient who has been hospitalized over 2 years. Yet every weekday, she "honors his humanity" by coming to visit and truly listen to him. I liked the draft questions. I would perhaps consider adding one about how to deal with burnout/compassion fatigue: how to stay compassionate when you are really tired?

Who are the people, ideas, or events that shaped your view on purpose and meaning? Primarily my mother. She was very active in the community. Also, my youngest sister Theresa who lives with Down Syndrome.

What do you see as your purpose? To bring human contact to people in the hospital so they feel that they are human as well as being a patient. Belongingness needs, Love needs and Self Esteem needs are just as important as the physical needs these people have. Basically, to Be Somebody Who Makes Everyone Feel like a Somebody.

What do you do to stay clear to your purpose? "I try to bring energy to work each day. I like to travel with my husband because that recharges my batteries. Reading and art help me stay focused.

What inspires you? My compassionate co-workers inspire me and offer me support when life gets difficult. Talking to them also gives me excellent ideas. Nature inspires me.

I think I would point to a nurse that I know in my life. Nursing as a profession, vocation or even a spiritual exercise is inspiring when done with ethics and virtue. We do not usually associate God with the diligence with which we perform our work. However, there can be a connection between the secular world of work and the sacred. In nursing spirituality is relevant to the performance of a nurse's work. The best nurses respond to their patients with compassion, dedication, and an excellent grasp of medical knowledge. Incompetence is not a virtue. You can be competent without compassion, but there is no spirituality in that state. All of us in our work can take value from including spirituality in our daily work effort. All work in this world is connected to toil and hardship. A statement from Vatican II tells us that workers rarely have an exclusive motive for what they are doing. They usually have different motives simultaneously. Accordingly, while nursing is away to earn living, it is also a way to serve humankind and at the same contributes to God's plan of continuing creation. May we all see strive to be our best at work and in our vocations, whatever they may be.

———

Hi Paul, I'll do my best to answer your questions from a 95-year-old's point of view. My eyes are failing so it may be hard to stay on the lines but here goes!!

When I was about five and a half, living in a happy home with parents and an older brother, the Great Depression hit. Dad, like everyone else, went to the bank to get his money. There wasn't any. He came home with check books and stationery for us to play with. This was my first experience with empathy. I call it sympathy. My Mom was crying, seemed like all the time, and I remember patting her lap and saying, "it will be okay." What does a kid know? Well, I've wandered far from the question.

I think my purpose in life was to raise two good, honest, and upright citizens. Though they are total opposites, I'm proud to say their mine. Each of them gave me three grandchildren. You know my son's. My daughter's two boys work for their Dad, driving trucks and working in the garage. They are best friends, seldom seeing one without the other.

Boy, my eyes are getting worse so I need to hurry up. They seem to get tired. I sure will be glad to get home to my specialist in two more weeks.

I'm inspired by other people, friends or relatives. I have the attitude that if they can do it, so can I. Of course, that's a "used to be" attitude. One of my favorite persons to inspire me was Steve who was one of my son's friends from his early college days. My son had a car at school and drove home often. He brought a friend with him who I can best describe as "mellow." He was a transcendental meditationalist. It wasn't long after he left that my husband and I paid the hundred dollars to learn how (heck, I could teach anyone if they were serious). Each of us had to take a new white men's handkerchief, a piece of fruit and a just-picked flower. Luckily, daffodils were in season. Separately, we were given a Mantra. No one else could know it. Mine was "Kerring." My husband never told me his. The word is to put you in a trance. Just keep repeating it until every sound around you is shut out. I can testify that it works. You can (actually?) leave your body. It's kind of scary. I haven't done it for years but I think I may start. Can't (hurt?) and I surely have time. My writing is getting pitiful but I have to tell you something funny happened out at Notre Dame one night. We used to go out there where we met other meditationalists. Of course, they were all highly educated and we are a couple of farmers. The person sitting next to me actually fell of his chair. I don't know if he was meditating or fell asleep, but he sure brought us to life!

That's the end of the story. Hi to Karen. I'm secretly hoping to make the trip again. I have days when I'm sure I could. And days when I say, "what were you thinking?"

Betty

———

Here's my interview with Fred Taylor, the first Executive Director of For Love of Children. First, by way of background, I'll include a brief introduction from John W. Anderson, long-time journalist and editorialist with the Washington Post on Fred:

"As a result of socio-economic changes, in the late 1950's and early 1960s, there was a large increase in the number of children in DC's main orphanage, DC Village. There was limited funding for the orphanage and as the number of children increased, the conditions for the children became radically worse. There were just enough resources to keep them from malnutrition, but the children were rarely talked to and didn't get any real affection. Children weren't learning to talk and grew up grossly deprived. Even back then, we knew about the devastating impact of lack of affection on children.

The Washington Post did a series of investigative reports on the conditions at DC Village. I was on the editorial board from around 1961- 1965. During that time, I wrote repeated editorials about DC Village.

Fred Taylor, God Bless him, read the articles and took action.

All the serious work was done by Fred – organizing, fundraising, finding foster homes for the children. Finding homes for the hundreds of children was very difficult.

Over the years, FLOC tried several different things to try to develop long-term solutions to problems encountered by the youth of the District of Columbia. Over a period of considerable time, FLOC figured out supporting educational help and moral support to the children of the District of Columbia was the most important thing it could do and it has done so admirably for over fifty years.

In retrospect, those stories I wrote may have been the most impactful of all the things I did in my career.

I have the highest respect for Fred Taylor, I can honestly say that there is nobody on the planet who did more for the children of the District of Columbia." (John Anderson)

OK, so here's the interview:

My parents influenced me greatly in a positive manner. My Dad was a retail lumber dealer. Being part of the community and active in the community was important to him. The kids didn't have anything to do in the summer. Dad led the community to raise $2,000 for equipment and a staff person for two months to provide a summer recreation program. A local school teacher owed him $1,500 - my Dad got him to fill in a sink hole in a field, plow an infield and made a baseball diamond. My Dad then started a children's softball team. A few years later, when my brother and I complained about nothing to do with summer approaching, Dad pulled high school athletes together to form a softball league and rented a lot for the games.

That's an example of satisfying a family need in a way that all the town kids could benefit. My Dad was my model for "servant leadership."

Gordon Cosby was another major influence in my life. Gordon was the founder and pastor of the Church of the Savior.

Gordon was instrumental in creating the movement and organization together to address a critical community need to stop the warehousing of neglected and homeless child in the 900-bed institution known as Junior Village.

Gordon "called it together," asked me to build the organization that became For Love of Children (FLOC) with lots of volunteers from his Church of the Savior.

Gordon was also instrumental in helping me find my calling. I went to Gordon for counseling. He told me that "sometimes you're in a place that is not calling out your gifts" and you need to "go to a neutral place to recall." Gordon had a way of "calling people for their gifts," gifts they didn't know they had. He did this for me and I've tried to do this for others.

After I gave up my ministry, I took a job with a federally funded D.C. job training program. I was there only a year but it was a rich year. In this experience, I was "baptized in the African American culture." I felt so happy after experiencing true misery in a place in which I didn't fit (my ministry). I started attending the Church of the Savior. Gordon Cosby was part of a coalition looking for a full-time Director, which started with a single purpose - to close Junior Village.

I see as my purpose to serve God as best I understand. I see this as the role of a servant leader.

I consider relationships starting from the family and moving out to be the greatest gift and proving ground of my faith.

I try to stay clear to your purpose through persistence, humility, and recognizing and learning from the mistakes.

I deal with compassion fatigue by realizing that I have to take care of myself if I am to be able to care of others. I have a great support system with my family. Also, I try to have fun at the same time I try to "make things happen."

I am inspired by the people I have worked with at FLOC, its many partners and people we serve. Over FLOC's fifty plus years, there have been countless times when an extraordinary person has arrived or stepped up in a time of need to keep this organization headed in the right direction. I also draw inspiration from learning about the lives of public figures, particularly U.S. presidents. There is so much to learn about leadership from reading their biographies and autobiographies. Just recently, a few Presidents I have read about include Teddy Roosevelt, Abraham Lincoln, John Quincy Adams, and Andrew Jackson.

———

Of purpose and meaning, my life was filled with God-conscious people: my immediate family who were daily Mass-goers and my nun-teachers who taught me from first grade through college and remained my friends all my life. I learned early on life was all about God.

Of empathy, the kind, selfless, caring people God placed in my life all along. I sorely needed them because I was an odd child whom many people often found difficult to accept. My personality was a built-in sieve. Only the Christ-like could accept me so my life was filled with Christ-like people whose goodness I got by osmosis.

I see as my purpose to do what God wills me to do from moment to moment.

I try to stay clear to my purpose by paying attention to God, namely by praying.

I am inspired by goodness, caring, kindness, joy, beauty, peace, persistence and enthusiasm for the things that are God's.

I don't experience burnout or compassion fatigue? I see myself as a conduit of God's compassion channeling it to the person in need of it. Have you ever heard of a tired water pipe? All it really does is lie there for the water to come through it. In time, the pipe wears out as I will when I die. In the meantime, the Lord's compassion is welcome to keep coming through me to someone who needs it.

Or to use another image. A young seminarian was telling me about his compassion fatigue. I told him that I think of a person in distress as someone on rolling skates carrying the largest trash can filled with wet manure. When they come to us for help we are not meant to take that trash can from them and carry it for them. We are just meant to take it from them and set it down on the ground since their being on roller skates prevents them from doing that without risking a major debacle. They simply need our objectivity, our listening, our caring and our prayers.

The Holy Cross girls taught me that. When I was set to offer them solutions to their problems, they said: "Don't say anything, Mrs. J. Just listen to me!" Which I did. And when the bell rang, they ran off raving, "Thanks so much! I feel so much better!" I have come to believe that maybe as much as wisdom, the person who needs empathy simply needs us to be present to them. That I am able to give them. It is my way of honoring and paying back all those who gave me their time and caring when I was in need of both.

I hope this is the feedback you were looking for from me. God richly bless your efforts for our next book

(L. Jardeleza)

———

My Friend Ken: I've known Ken for several years. We came to know each other through our mutual parish and related events.

We're connected in several ways – close in age, similar family structures and common social environments. But most of what I know about Ken has been learned from observations and brief but meaningful conversations.

While working on this writing project, I noticed that Ken seemed to have an increased ability and capacity for empathy. I tuned into it through his actions toward me. He always made it a point to check in on my condition. "How are things?" was more than a dismissive question as most of us treat it. He really wanted to know. And when the answer wasn't rainbows and unicorns, he wanted to help. Then helped. For example, when I lost my job after nearly 16 years, Ken was there every step of the way. First to empathize – just checking in on feelings – "Doing ok?", "How's the job search going?" But Ken took action too – making connections, hunting down job openings, giving words of encouragement... It was welcome but I wondered how much he put into this effort. After all, I knew that Ken needed some of this too. I wasn't sure that I deserved what he was giving me. I felt greedy – there were certainly others who needed this more than me – an older gentleman battling cancer or the one navigating health issues and the trauma of divorce. But Ken did it for the others too. On several occasions he must have been directing his empathy towards multiple people and I often wondered how he could do that. How he could help so many people and still have the capacity for attention to his family and his own needs?

I had the opportunity to spend a weekend camping trip Ken and our respective daughters. I took the opportunity so share the book that resulted in the writing of this very sentence – "What Have We Learned So Far?" Ken is more spiritual than I am, and he welcomed the gesture and was genuinely interested in my writing project. We talked a bit about life's challenges and our approaches to self-improvement. We concluded that self-improvement is a prerequisite to improvement in our family and society.

I wondered what made Ken this way – so willing and able to practice empathy in a very real way. In my conversations with him and I suspect it is this way for many of us – the ability and the drive come from some common sources. A family – either children or at least some close-knit family or social group and the desire to have a positive impact on those around us. There is also a commitment to beliefs that are present. This could be influenced by religion, but I think mostly derives from our personal beliefs that happen to align with a religion or particular set of values. And finally, there was are one or more triggers – life experiences – that cause us to arrive at the starting point on our empathy journey. The details of those experiences don't matter much, it's what we do with them that will set our direction in life. Those of us like Ken gravitate towards using their gift to do good and make a positive impact on the lives of others. This in turn help to fulfil the needs of the individual whether they know it or not. In other words, some of us need to practice empathy in order to thrive or at least pursue spiritual fulfillment. Where are we on addressing the needs of Maslow's hierarchy? LOL. Our journey along the path of empathy can address our needs on several of the levels.

More important than the job postings or connections that were given to me by Ken and others was the gift of empathy that was shared with me. It allowed me to become more aware of my abilities to positively impact others and grow my own capacity for empathy. I was certainly given more than I felt I deserved, but I'm now inclined to pay it forward and do the same for others. It's a virtuous cycle and I'm grateful for everyone around me whether family, friends, acquaintances or strangers, that is willing and able to look after me. I hope I can do the same in my life and teach others through my good example.

———

Who are the people, ideas, or events that shaped your view on purpose and meaning? My Grandfather. He was the hardest working man I had ever seen. He always had time for his kids, grandkids, and helping those in the community. The book: "*Choice Theory – The New Real-*

ity Therapy", by William Glasser, taught me very simple, but complex outlook in life. All you grasp in your life is your own choices. You will never control anyone else's circle. I have made mistakes in life and pushed myself to overcome my failures and it's led me to personal success in life. Being poor taught me value, to work hard, always give 100%, and be grateful for those in my life and the blessings I have. My Family and Friends give me meaning - some gauge wealth with a dollar sign. I value wealth in sharing experiences with friends and family. I see the joy gathering brings to my family and to those around me. My Parents strongly shaped my views. They were divorced when I was young. My father left and it put my family through some hardships. My mother stepped up and did what she had to do for my sister and I to sustain. I looked up to her. My Dad has made reparations and we have mended our relationship.

What do you see as your purpose? To be the best me I can be every day. Be honest and live with integrity. I know I will have off days, but if I approach the day with positivity and be the best dad, husband, friend, and person I can be I know my actions can and will impact the lives of those around me. I try to stay positive even if there is negativity. I understand that people have a lot going on in their lives. There are millions of points in peoples' lives that shape who they are, how they think, and how they act. I approach people with this in mind. I try not to say no. I find some of the best rewards in life come with saying yes.

What do you do to stay clear to your purpose? Take it one day at a time. Never stop learning, be kind and thoughtful for those around you. Also, I value my faith. I make time to pray mostly every day. Even on days I don't accomplish much, I feel that praying for the people in my life who need it most is an easy way to give back for the good things I have in my life.

What inspires you? My family and friends. I love people, I love spending time with people. Laughter is always the best medicine. God as well. I have met some really fantastic people through my faith. I enjoy going to mass and participating in the parish. I love to take care of others.

Have you had to deal with burnout/compassion fatigue? How do you stay compassionate when you are really tired? Yes. I do get down, upset, and angry at times. Lifting weights and working out is a good outlet to blow off steam. On occasion, I do argue/fight with the ones I love. It's not all rainbows and butterflies. I stay compassionate again, because I don't know what's going on in the minds of those around me. Even my wife or those who are closest to me. There are a million things or moments in their lives I don't know about. You never know when those moments are affecting them. When people have off days, cut them some slack. I do believe there is a limitation to this concept though. Sometimes there are just some bad seeds or people who just do not bring value to a relationship. I feel the largest failures in society are those who have been failed by their family. Everyone is born with an assemblance of a moral compass. However learning to make good choices is not something everyone inherits. For instance, one of the issues that burns me out is the violence in Chicago. A few years back, there was a teenage African American boy and his friend in one of the more rough neighborhoods in Chicago. They encounter an older African American man in his seventies watering his lawn. They teens robbed the older man and decided to murder him. Their take was $20. These boys were so devoid of emotion and moral assemblance that they put the value of someone's life at $20. I struggle to see the way these kids have been failed. I understand the kid made the choice to take another person's life for $20, but the amount of failure this kid has endured has to be insurmountable. Or maybe it's not. Instances like this hit me with a sense of burnout. Also, I feel the media, movies, entertainment, and society are overstepping their bounds. I stay away from social media. I feel like social media has taken the instant gratification society to the next level. Generally, I don't care to hear negative news. I know it's out there, but I want the good news. It seems these outlets these days force feed negativity or the need to change people's thoughts and behavior. I think regardless of where you stand politically, socio-economically, we all have pretty similar needs and wants in life. The problem lies within us (humans) and being selfish. We try to force others to see the world in our way. Rather than focus on what we have in common, agree that we will not always agree, and cope with one another. Have more compassion, understanding in the fact that we all do not prioritize ideas, beliefs, and experiences in the same manner. But knowing this will likely not be the case or the next agenda for the right or left to push gives me grief. I know we could do better, but too many folks are focused on forcing controlling one another instead of focusing on control themselves and being better versions of ourselves.

———

Hi Paul - the people that I am inspired by are the people I serve here because no matter what their circumstances are that continue to try to move forward to better their lives. My parents and my grandmother shaped m because as child I always had a natural gift of wanting to help people do better. My family always taught me that knowledge is power and it was important to be informed and to share experiences.

I think my purpose is to help people do better in life. I always push forward along with having the mindset that I might not be able to help all but if I can help one and/or some, I am clear on my purpose. People are my inspiration - both adults and children. When I get burned out I have to take a break, go exercise, do something social with family and/or friends, or take a vacation. When it gets to that point you have to focus on self-wellness and care because we are all human with emotions. When I take a break from burnout I return feeling more energized but all so keeping in mind I might not be able help "everybody" but I can sure make a difference with some.

(Kim G)

————

Who are the people, ideas, or events that shaped your view on purpose and meaning? Several years ago, I asked my husband what he had wanted to be when he grew up. After thinking about it for a few moments, he said that he'd wanted "to be good."

It was an answer that resonated with me. Growing up in a single-parent home, I became increasingly aware of, and sensitive to, the toll that my father's departure (when I was three and my sister was one) was taking on my mother. An English teacher, she spent most evenings correcting papers, making clothes for herself, my sister, and me, and falling asleep on the sofa, exhausted. Despite being (what I now know to be) depressed, her standards were exacting. She never missed a day of work except for when she was in the hospital, and she was known for being an extremely strict teacher (a quality unappreciated by her students—as well as by some of their parents). Years later, however, it was heartening to me to witness so many of her former students come up to her to tell her that her teaching made all the difference in their ability to write well.

My mother also took civic responsibilities very seriously, playing the organ at two local churches every week for decades (refusing payment for her services), gave piano lessons to several neighborhood children weekly (payment for which was ear-marked for the church and kept in a covered basket on top of the piano), as well as participating in a Prayer Group that met weekly at the homes of its participants, Eastern Star, North Country Chorus, and Delta Kappa Gamma (an organization of teachers). Despite having very little money (when, after teaching for 40 years, she retired, her salary was $14,000), she ensured that both my sister and I went to (and graduated from) college. Although I don't recall my mother ever saying a word about us getting married or having children someday, we were taught, from childhood, that we needed to find something (i.e., not someone) to make us happy.

What do you see as your purpose and how do you stay clear to your purpose?
Having written the above, I'm a bit stunned by the extent to which my sister and I seemed to follow my mother's lead. Neither my sister nor I ever seemed to have a desire to have children and

both of us were very "iffy" about getting married. (Fortunately, lessons learned during a first marriage paid off—in unimaginable ways—in a wonderfully satisfying and illuminating second marriage!) We did, however, throw ourselves into our studies, went to college, and found a home in service professions—my sister, as a Special Education teacher working with those who had developmental delays; I, as an art therapist working with children with emotional disturbances and, as a teacher of students studying to become art therapists. So, in sum, I believe that both my sister and I might say that our purpose lay in finding ways of being of service, whether it takes the form of listening to someone who is in need of understanding or consists of the passing on of skills that might be useful.

What inspires you? So much: nature, reading, the examples of others. Just last week, at a conference, I had the opportunity to hear Essam Daod, MD, a Palestinian psychiatrist, talk about the work of an international organization that he co-founded, Humanity Crew, that provides psychological aid to refugees, beginning with rescuing them from overly laden boats at sea.

Have you had to deal with burnout/compassion fatigue? How do you stay compassionate when you are really tired? Since I tend to rely upon compartmentalization, a practice I initiated at the beginning of my working life was to endeavor—while I was taking the bus to work—to push back (i.e., towards "home") any thoughts/concerns I had about home life and—while I was taking the bus home—to push back (towards the work place) any thoughts/concerns I had about work. I hoped that this would allow me to be as fully present as possible while I was at work and while I was at home.

I also instituted the practice of relaxing in a bath as soon as I got home from work, visualizing—as the tub emptied--all the cares of work disappearing down the drain, releasing me for whatever arose in my personal time. This worked fairly well over the nearly 30 years that I worked at a psycho-educational facility.

I'm also a firm believer in the restorative effects of massage!

———

Who are the people, ideas, or events that shaped your view on purpose and meaning? I am the sum of my parents, friends and neighbors, teachers, coaches, mentors, managers, and colleagues who have offered guidance, direction, admonition and encouragement over my life and career. I have filtered those inputs as I have lived, making adjustments as needed, adapting as required.

What do you see as your purpose? My first purpose is to provide for my wife and daughters: a home, education, value input, comfortable lifestyle while, to the best of my ability, contributing time and resources to others less fortunate. We have been able to do that.

What do you do to stay clear to your purpose? To those ends, I focused on my education by which to prepare and qualify me for the best job possible. Along the way, I continued my education to adapt to the increasing use of technology and skills related to managing and leading teams with purpose and sensitivity to each as individuals. Over that period of time, cultural milestones have occurred to force that adaptation. Perhaps most importantly, the status of women changed dramatically from being 'property' with little opportunity beyond teaching, nursing or secretarial work to the fully participative roles not only across every industry and government sector, including military service, but into leadership roles that included Board Chair and President/CEO. This motivated us as parents to guide our daughters into college study that prepared them for full participation in this new normal, something in which we take immense pride. This in turn has resulted in their true parental and marital partnerships in raising our grandchildren. We treasure family and all the tests that come with it. While we are religious, we are not maniacal or blindly following the church's teachings. We are not above sacrificing some work-life balance to achieve career objectives, taking a longer term view in doing so. Our values guide our decision making to what is generally accepted as right versus wrong, bending along the way, patriotic with reasoned questioning of authority and suspicion of those too long in office, and holding ourselves accountable for our actions and decisions rather than blaming someone or something else. We feel very strongly that each day, we must be able to look at ourselves in the mirror and at each other and like what we see. We see increasing grass-roots activism to an extent that did not exist in my youth. That has somewhat reduced the unilateral decision-making of those elected but has clouded the concept of the right direction since consensus is often a casualty.

What inspires you? I look at our grandchildren, how they have grown, the successes they have achieved and the people they have become, and I conclude that we have accomplished a great deal. I look at our daughters and sons-in-law and smile inwardly at the adults they are, their devotion to community, the causes they support, the way they treat each other and us, and I conclude that this is inspirational beyond what we imagined when we decided to marry. I am inspired at acts of kindness and selflessness, courage in the face of intimidating and life-threatening circumstances and people's abilities to persevere. I am inspired when underdogs and the under-estimated rise to accomplish what others, and often they themselves, did not expect.

Have you had to deal with burnout/compassion fatigue? Not often. To the extent that I have been able to provide relief to those in need, I consider it part of my role rather than something for which to be congratulated or thanked. I do it because it is the right thing to do. The burnout or fatigue is the result of taking on more than capabilities or time allow, something I have managed well.

How do you stay compassionate when you are really tired? A good night's sleep often recharges my batteries to restore the compassion and energy to continue the plan to conclusion. During the day, taking the time to reflect, even for a few minutes, helps restore perspective toward good decision-making.

———

Here is my interview with Myra Woolery Antill, Pediatric Clinical Nurse Specialist and Head of Camp Fantastic for as long as I remember:

Who are the people, ideas, or events that shaped your view on purpose and meaning? My coworkers, the kids I work with and their parents. Seeing the incremental and massive strides we have made in treating pediatric cancer and HIV makes me feel like I am doing something to help make the world a better place.

What do you see as your purpose? The reality is that it's sad to see sick children. My purpose is to make their journey through this difficult experience a little less miserable. There are times that are really hard for a nurse. However, there's also so much joy in my specialty. I have kids whom I've followed since they were little. I've had the privilege of watching them grow up.

What do you do to stay clear to your purpose? One of the things that's great about our team is that we support each other emotionally and spiritually through the difficult times. We remind each other what this job, what our purpose, is all about. No one but another nurse will understand what it's like to lose a beloved patient. The colleague next to you can support you like no one else can. One of the reasons I love this specialty is the team. They do an excellent job of understanding where we each come from in facing these challenges. Our shared experiences, both difficult and joyful, strengthen our collective bond.

What inspires you? These children are normal kids in an abnormal situation. Being witness to their lives and their strength is an amazing experience. I feel inspired seeing the fortitude of the kids we work with. Kids who deal with chronic or life-threatening diagnoses have an inner strength that's incredible to see in people who are so young. It's an honor to work with them and see their spirit and courage on a daily basis.

Have you had to deal with burnout/compassion fatigue? The main time in my life when I really had burnout was when my Mom got leukemia. I found I couldn't be a supportive daughter and good nurse at the same time. I was burning the candle at both ends and fulfilling neither role well. I had to take a leave of absence. It was probably about 3 months after she died that I felt able to give my job what it needed. I worry about nurses who don't have the ability to take a leave of absence when they need it. I worry about their patients.

How do you stay compassionate when you are really tired? My cats and my art are how I refill my "empathy tank."

———

And here are the responses from the team:

I'm going to frame my answer around climate change mainly because it is the biggest issue we are facing, but also because I think a lot of the other challenging problems of our humanity can be tackled while also solving climate change. I took an Oceanography class taught by Bruce Monger in college, and because I did not attend all (or most) of the classes, I had the unique opportunity of listening to all the class recordings online at about double the speed in approximately 10 hours. Besides the unnerving ocean-related dreams narrated by a speedy professor that plagued my finals week, the thought that remained in my brain until this day is the main point the professor consistently made throughout the semester (or in my case, one night): that we are the generation of people who will either save our planet and its inhabitants, or doom it for 10,000 years. How horrifying! It's US. Why the heck are we the ones who have to deal with this? Or are we special because we were born at this time? I like to think that we are special. That we are the generation that will forever be known as the people who SAVED everything. Up until this point, no human on the history of Earth has ever faced something so important. We decide the fate of our planet for the next 10,000 years. This isn't as simple as deciding not to do something, like not to bomb our entire planet. This is a decision that the entire planet will have to come together to actively make and carry out. So what do we (collectively) need to do to move in the right direction? I am going to reference my Oceanography professor again. He made the point that we are not going to make any real difference by recycling our amazon boxes; instead, we need change to happen in leadership. The most important thing an individual can do to help solve climate change is to vote. Once we have proper leadership we can focus on coming together as a whole planet to solve climate change.

In history, we've seen how humans will unite through collective desires and efforts, for example, a 2nd grade class trying to get an extra 5 minutes of recess, a stadium full of fans rooting on their football team, a country trying to reach the next undiscovered frontier, a group of countries fighting together in a war. Our current world seems especially divided despite our technological advances in communication. Perhaps that's why our planet has a built-in self-destruct mechanism for when we don't get along, we don't think about how advancing ourselves will affect smaller communities, we don't care about all of the effects of our ignorance, and we don't listen to the experts formed through our own education systems. You might think, well I do all of those things, I care! Well good for you, me too. Unfortunately, not all the current leaders do. I was never a huge fan of History as a subject in school. I used to roll my eyes every time a teacher said, "we need to learn History so it doesn't repeat itself". Well, I guess I change my mind, because there have been some amazing examples in history of humans coming together to accomplish something seemingly impossible. I think we all crave that feeling of being part of something bigger than ourselves. Well imagine that "something" is literally an effort to save our entire planet. I mean, there is nothing bigger that we can even do (at least not yet). This is not the plot of a "save the world" book or movie, this is reality! How amazing is that? What do you think will happen in the end? Will this be one of those depressing books the guy in a tie at book club would pick, or will it be the story kids grow up wishing they could be in: the one where we save the world and everyone lives happily ever after? I certainly hope the latter! And I also hope that once we all come together to accomplish solving climate change, that we will be inherently unified as a species. Being part of something bigger than ourselves helps people become more empathetic on an individual scale by understanding the things that unite us all together. And as change does happen, I think we will be exposed to more and more instances of both terrible effects of climate change, as well as amazing examples of humans showing compassion for one another. I think that this exposure will naturally cause people to feel more empathetic as things progress.

I was really excited at the prospect of asking someone about their beliefs and I started thinking about who I wanted to interview. I had someone in mind, but I realized I genuinely wanted to know what many people saw as their purpose in life. I asked 18 people (people not already participating in this project) ranging from ages 17 to 80s same question: "What do you see as your purpose in life?" Whether that purpose has anything to do with saving the climate change crisis, I wanted to know if people even had a sense of purpose and if they did, whether there were any unifying patterns... Here were the answers:

"To live a long and happy life and leave the world better than I found it."

"My purpose in life is to be a kind, caring, helpful, and compassionate person to those around me and to raise my children to be the same - to be good to one another!"

"There is probably a purpose, I just haven't seen it yet. And I believe that those who try to actively search for one hardly ever find their true purpose. It just comes naturally, ya feel?"

"To make people laugh, brighten other people's days, and be a strong moral example for others"

"I'm not sure we will ever know what our purpose is, although there has to be something. I think regardless of what belief system you have, you're supposed to be civil and nice because you don't want to hurt other people. For me specifically, again I can't know my whole purpose for sure, but it includes raising children and making them feel loved and secure, as well as taking care of my parents."

"To help the ocean and be around the ocean because if someone else doesn't help, then it's likely that a lot of stuff is going to die."

"To make the world a better place, I'm just not sure how."

"Every person has a soul. There is a God or a divine being, and our purpose is to do His/Her will. If there is no such 'divine being', we are no different from any other animal. I don't think my purpose is a unique purpose, it is to love and serve God and live a moral and good life."

"I think my purpose in life is to create. I find joy and fulfillment in creating whether it be writing, dancing, singing, etc. I find that I've been not only been able to feel joy through creating, but I've also been able to bring others joy through creating."

"Build awesome stuff, leave the place better than I found it, and enjoy the ride. That last bit involves finding and spending time with people I love."

"Because God created us in His image and likeness, we have that Godliness in us, and Jesus showed us how to express it through His example. It is up to us to use our own talents to enhance the lives of others. My purpose is to be the best mom, best teacher, and the best in anything I try because God gave me those talents and He wants me to use them to make others happy, content, and inspired."

"To help the helpless, animals, and the environment. They have no say in our world, but they need protecting, especially now. Most big businesses would rather save a penny and hurt the environment 10 times more than worry about the environment. My purpose is to help them to make sure they survive in the greedy world humans have created."

"To provide compassion to every human especially those in need. To look for the good in situations and try to lift others with a positive perspective."

"To help enrich society and make the world a bit better than when I arrived in it."

"I think the idea of each individual life having a purpose is kind of silly. We all have been given the gift of life and I'd prefer to spend my time exploring what inspires me rather than unsuccessfully trying to track down my 'predetermined path'. But I find that the most rewarding things to be those that challenge me the most, because they force me to grow as well. Or when I volunteer, *because those tasks normally wouldn't get done if me and my cohorts didn't take interest in the cause. I positively impact people through volunteering, mentoring, and teaching."*

"To enhance the way that people engage in dialogue to lead to better solutions to things."

"Who made you? God made me! Why did God make you? To know Him, love Him, and serve Him in this life and to be with Him in the next! I guess we should do the best we can with whatever talents and special traits we have been given. Life is very short, and I haven't spent a lot of time trying to figure it out. I've just tried to enjoy the time I was given here."

"To make a substantial, positive impact on a few people's lives, and a minor, positive impact on a lot of peoples' lives."

"I think one of my purposes in life is connecting with and supporting others through acts of kindness, understanding, a listening ear, and an open heart."

It was so interesting to see how people responded, not just the words. Some people responded immediately, as if this is a question they are continuously thinking about and updating. Others seemed stressed at the idea of having to consider their answer, as if this answer is something they think defines them as a person. Several people expressed that they weren't accustomed to thinking so deeply. Regardless of whether I received a response immediately or had to wrangle it out of people, I found that the responses were all incredibly thought-provoking. I wouldn't say I predicted any of these answers based on the person. Many responses have to do with morality and making the world a better place, but specific to that person's talents and interests. Others express the unknown associated with our purpose, which I am sure everyone has felt. Some touch on religion (predominantly Christianity due to selection bias), showing that the sense of purpose extends to something that is bigger than us.

I love the response that says "I find that I've been not only able to feel joy through creating, but I've also been able to bring others joy through creating" for two main reasons: 1. because I found that although I wanted to inspire other people to think deeply, they ended up inspiring me, and 2. because I think the notion that our purpose in life has to somehow be painful or unenjoyable work isn't right. We all have our own unique passions and talents, which we can use to influence others for the better. I think it's beautiful that we are all so unique. That gives us the opportunity to work with the rest of humanity by relying on some and helping others. We can find fulfillment in understanding and appreciating everyone's own unique contribution to humanity. And I think that's what the goal of empathy is.

(Samantha)

———

"People become builders by building and lyre players by playing the lyre; so too do we become just by doing just acts, temperate by doing temperate acts, brave by doing brave acts." (Aristotle as quoted by Wendy Wood in "Good Habits; Bad Habits")

It has been a lifelong struggle for me to balance action and contemplation. Both seem essential. I consciously chose my career path because I wanted my work to be of use to individuals and to the community. Between my work and raising my family, action was the dominant "way" for most of my life, but now that I am mostly retired, the contemplative way has become increasingly important. I do continue to spend at least one day a week in my active work role. What this second project has made me realize is that I have a responsibility to become informed on the issues that impact so heavily on the lives of the marginalized and vulnerable, e.g., immigration, our criminal justice system, racism, etc. I would like to quote from "The New Jim Crow" (p.241). "More than forty-five years ago, Martin Luther King Jr. warned . . . that blindness and indifference to racial groups is actually more important than racial hostility to the creation and maintenance of radicalized systems of control. Those who supported slavery and Jim Crow, he argued, typically were not bad or evil people; they were just blind. Even the Justices who decided the infamous Dred Scott case, which ruled *"that the Negro has no rights which the white man is bound to respect,"* were not wicked men, he said. On the contrary, they were decent and dedicated men. But, he hastened to add, *"They were victims of a spiritual and intellectual blindness. They knew not what they did. The whole system of slavery was largely perpetuated through spiritually ignorant persons. . .What a tragedy! Millions of Negroes have been crucified by conscientious blindness."*

So if I allow myself in remain in ignorance, I am acting and choosing to remain part of the problem rather than part of the solution. As I become more aware of how our current policies, customs and culture are discriminatory and oppressive, I am wrestling with what it is that I need to do. Empathy is an essential initial step. Unless I can try to understand how people are hurting and how the "system" (formal or informal) is exacerbating the hurt, I won't be moved to act. As I interpret Aristotle's words at the beginning and try to apply them to my life, I think it means that I should consciously, and with empathy, act in ways that contribute to making our community/country/world move in the direction of love for everyone and for our environment. It is only by continued practice that I can hope to become reliably just and helpful.

(Trudy)

———

Can you make a person feel empathy? At first thought my answer is "Yes, but only about things they already care about." So, if someone cares greatly about their car, I may invoke empathy by sharing a car trouble I'm having. However, the same person may be heartless and cold when presented with my cat's health problems. They simply can't relate. Others, I've found, seem to dole out empathy to those they feel "deserve" it. If you say "I feel badly that Kim Kardashian was robbed and tied up in her own house," you will get a mix of replies, many of which focus on Kim's wealth and the fact that the robbery made almost no impact on her net worth. However, if the same thing happens to non-wealthy person, and even if nothing is stolen, most people would feel empathy, acknowledging the psychological trauma that will haunt that person for the rest of their lives. Kim Kardashian has been public about the psychological trauma she still endures from the event, but is she not entitled to the same empathy given to others "less fortunate"?

In the internet world, there are several public figures who are revered as Heroes. These people include Steve Irwin, Bob Ross, and Mr. Rogers. If you search the internet for memes about these gentlemen, you will discover the impossible: comment sections with ZERO negative comments. If you've EVER been on the internet, you will understand that this is a nearly impossible feat. It has become popular to regard these men as the absolute best examples of human decency. Littering, crocodile-skin wearing, meat-lovers are not exempt from the global esteem held for Steve Irwin, although you'd think they would be. Steve's passion for wildlife was infectious, and his message of wildlife conservation was inclusive. That same topic is utterly divisive in political conversations. How did Steve do it?

I can remember being 5 or 6 years old and watching Steve admire a tarantula - he picked up the extremely dangerous creature saying, "Aren't you a beauty!" Could I relate to that? Absolutely not! Though a Steve Irwin fanatic, I do not have any desire to pick up a tarantula, yet Steve's passion was real and contagious, and for some reason, made me want to feel that way too. So, I would like to revise my previous answer. I don't think you have to care about something already in order to feel empathy, because I simply did not care about that tarantula, yet I could relate to the way Steve looked at the creature, and how he picked it up so carefully - it's like how I picked up my new kittens, or how I held my cousins when they were first born. Mr. Rogers is quoted as saying, "There's a world of difference between insisting on someone's doing something and establishing an atmosphere in which that person can grow into wanting to do it." I think this gets at the heart of Steve Irwin's allure to both kids and adults alike. After spending an episode up close and personal with some of the most dangerous and hated creatures on the earth, Steve would end the show saying something like *"This crocodile's habitat, as well as many others', is being destroyed by humans who want to live in the area. But this mama deserves a home for her and her babies just as much as you and I do. I am proud of my team today that got this croc to safety, and I know with your help, we can save these beautiful creatures and their homes so that our children get to see them too.*" I think if we deliver messages like that, in which we invite people to grow, we might just encourage people into being more empathetic.

A few weeks back I was talking to a friend who was adopted as a baby. She has struggled throughout her life with her identity but recently came to the conclusion that what she desires most is a feeling of Community. I had a shiver go through my spine when the said that. There's a quote that my dad loves, "We are all in the same boat, upon a stormy sea, and we owe each other a terrible and tragic loyalty." That quote made an impression on me as well, although it seems a little abstract. I feel it most acutely when I come across another human while hiking through the woods. Although you would not say hi to every person you walk by in New York City, you almost always say hi to the other hiker, as if we don't normally have time to acknowledge another human's worth, but we will when it's staring us in the face and making us uncomfortable. Or maybe it's the surprise of coming across another human when we haven't seen on in a while that excites us. In reality, the fact that we come across any organisms out of all the (possibly infinite) life in the universe, that we can communicate with, that can understand our pain and our joy and can even share those emotions out of concern for us, is incredible.

I don't know exactly why we owe each other a terrible loyalty, but I think that's part of the message. There's no particular reason, there's nothing about a person that makes them more deserving of loyalty than any other. It is simply an inherent worth that every human has, that makes them "worthy" of empathy and loyalty with one another. Another quote from Mr. Rogers: "*The world needs a sense of worth, and it will achieve it only by its people feeling that they are worthwhile. Try your best to make goodness attractive. That's one of the toughest assignments you'll ever be given.*" Open yourself up to discovering a community in common that you have with each person. Not "Democrat" or "Republican," but maybe something like "Loves Their Family," or "Enjoys the crunch of snow beneath their feet," or even communities like "Suffering from Depression," or "Dealing with a Loss". Once you consider that humans are much more alike in their experiences of love, joy, and pain than they are different, I think empathy is a natural thing that follows. Think about the trillions of trees, weeds, fungi, and bacteria living in the woods - out of the trillions of organisms in those woods only 2 are capable of feeling empathy for each other.

So I think that's my advice: Consider the Community. Recognize that the loyalty you owe to others is the same loyalty that is owed to you, or to your family members, or to anyone you consider the most deserving (whether it's Steve Irwin, your Mother, or your pet).

Last quote by Mr. Rogers (man, is that guy quotable!): "*The connections we make in the course of a life - maybe that's what heaven is.*"

(Jennifer)

———

What do we (collectively) need to do to move in the right direction? First...As a general rule, I answer specific questions but I do not generally feel competent to give anyone advice. I would say that the primary thing that we need to do is just make a big effort to be more kind to each other. To remember basic rules of courtesy even when it seems like they no longer apply. Michelle Obama said "*When they go low, we go high.*" Her husband said "*Learning to stand in somebody else's shoes, to see through their eyes, that's how peace begins. And it's up to you to make that happen. Empathy is a quality of character that can change the world.*"

What role does empathy have in the direction we should take? I think that a primary purpose of human life is to serve; to show compassion and a willingness to help each other. Perhaps my favorite quote about empathy comes from arguably my favorite book- *To Kill a Mockingbird* by Harper Lee. Scout is mystified by her teacher and has justifiably attacked a little boy in her first grade class. Atticus Finch tells his daughter: "*If you can learn a simple trick, Scout, you'll get along a lot better with all kinds of folks. You never really understand a person until you consider things from his point of view, until you climb inside of his skin and walk around in it."*

What are you (the advice giver) doing now or going forward to help us move in the right direction? Not nearly enough, and clearly, not always the most effective actions. I am not always successful, but

I try to be a decent person, I try to be kind to my patients, I try to treat people the way I want to be treated, I try to do some worthwhile volunteer work, I try to donate to good causes, I vote, and I try to raise kids who are decent humans who will do something small to make the world a better place.

What recommendation do you have to the advice seeker about how to help us collectively move in the right direction? Find something that inspires you, that you are truly passionate about, a wrong that really needs to be righted and then do your little piece. Find someone who inspires you and let them inspire you and share their story with other people. The civil rights activist Claudette Colvin why, as a 15 year old, did she participate in the Montgomery, Alabama bus strike.

"Whenever people ask me "Why didn't you get up when the bust driver asked you?" I say it felt as though Harriet Tubman's hands were pushing me down on one shoulder and Sojourner Truth's hands were pushing me down on the other shoulder. I felt inspired by these women because my teacher taught us about them in so much detail." So....Claudette Colvin moved in the right direction not just because of the famous Harriet Tubman

and Sojourner Truth, who we have all heard of, but also because of a teacher we've never heard of.

(Therese)

———

As we approach the conclusion of our discussions on empathy, I am confident that what I've learned on this journey will leave me with a springboard for action. After all, empathy isn't passive. It can and should be engaging and active. When presented with a situation where exercising our empathy skills is required, one action we have the option to pursue is to give advice. And giving advice is likely the first thing most of us do to practice empathy.

I'm not sure that it should be the first step, however. The first step should involve listening, understanding and asking questions. This will help you to determine whether advice giving is an appropriate next step. It may be that the individual you are speaking with isn't seeking advice. Whether or not you move on to giving advice, you'll form some opinions and formulate that advice in your head anyway as you ask yourself "what would I do in this situation?" If we've been in that situation ourselves, the answer to the question may come to mind quickly. If we haven't, we're still likely to formulate advice based on similar if not the same experiences or draw from what we know about the experiences of others or what we have learned in school and life.

We must approach the business of advice giving carefully if we are to benefit the advice seeker and thusly the advice giver. Asserting your opinions is not the same as giving advice. In today's world, dishing out opinions on social media masquerades for advice. Read the comments on any Facebook topic, especially political, religious or other delicate topics – everyone shouts their opinion and readily hands out advice. The quality of that advice is unknown. The advice giver might be making themselves feel good (smart, generous, noble) but has no idea what impact their advice might be having on an advice seeker on the other end of the internet – in a positive or negative way.

I could have avoided the preceding paragraph by stating that social media is not a good medium for sharing personal advice. For better or worse, it's how people communicate today – social media, text messages, email – we're "living life in the comments." Therefore, we must understand how to navigate those waters carefully.

What can we do to move in the right direction? We need a compass for the right direction. Your compass might be religion, meditation, reflection, awareness, or education. Take time to pause and bring your mind to focus on the people in your life, including yourself that are seeking direction (a possible indicator of an advice seeker).

Lead with empathy. A natural call to action along our path to empathy in practice is to give advice. But it is not the first step. We may not have advice to give immediately. Start with listening. Consider different perspectives. Be open to alternatives that differ from experientially based opinions. Ask questions, but do not react with advice.

You'll know when advice is an appropriate next step. It will be asked for either directly or indirectly. Be cognizant that there are different ways to give advice – telling someone what to do, how to behave, or how to feel is not always effective nor welcomed. Try to formulate your advice (for your own purpose and for the advice seeker) by asking questions of yourself first. How do you feel in this situation? What outcomes would you like to see? What do you want to change? Or simply, "How can I help?"

The advice seeker (it might be me) should keep an open mind and respect the advice that is given. Respect does not mean take the advice. It just means listening to and considering what is ultimately an opinion. This advice should not be given lightly. Advice should be given when the advice giver has committed to doing the same. In other words, practice what you preach – or change what you preach.

I've previously discussed what I feel is a limitation on my capacity to practice empathy. I think we all have limitations and perhaps some of us have surplus capacity at certain times. I often feel that I need more empathy in my direction than I can outwardly practice toward others.

What can I do? I am committing to increasing my capacity to practice empathy. I aim to do this by consciously seeking out opportunities to practice empathy. I'll take time during prayer, meditation, or reflection to think about others that may need a bit of empathy directed their way. I'll take small actions along the way such as reaching out to those I identity though simple gestures. I'll take time to listen and understand different perspectives. I'll give advice when it's appropriate and refrain from advice giving when not needed – I'll seek other impactful actions. I'll follow my own advice and be more self-aware when I am not walking the talk. My hope is that by increasing the practice, I will increase my capacity for empathy.

Why is this important to me? Empathy is a tool we can use to lift each other up. We can use it to lift ourselves up and give us direction and ultimately purpose. We use it lift us all up to be better together. It's clearly something we all need. If we all need it, then we have an obligation to practice empathy or risk missing its inherent benefits to both the individual and our society.

Empathy, and our capacity for it, is a gift. We should not take it for granted, practice empathy when we can and sharpen our abilities through actions (guided by empathy) to maximize the positive impact we can have on our lives and the lives of each other.

(Dan)

———

What do we (collectively) need to do to move in the right direction? The "right direction" is a highly individual concept that is colored by our own life's experiences, the way we were raised and educated, and the values we hold dear. My view is that this term will be defined differently by citizens versus non-citizens, offspring of military or government officials versus private sector folks, gender, age/generation, wealth or lack thereof, and education. In order to move in the right direction, there must be consensus on what that objective is. If it cannot be agreed upon and defined, we cannot proceed toward the plan to accomplish it. To quote the philosopher, Lawrence Peter Berra, *"if you don't know where you're going, you'll never get there."* We need to think collectively and too often today folks think parochially.

What role does empathy have in the direction we should take? Empathy recognizes the difficulties of some of the characteristics stated above. Empathy generally is commiseration with another's misfortunes or troubles with a demonstrable effort to help resolve them, particularly when the victim's emotional or intellectual state is so consumed with those difficulties that s/he is at least temporarily unable to work through to a resolution themselves....my apologies for my inability to correctly pronoun the multiple genders. As this direction may involve politics, it becomes incumbent upon those who have empathy for others to proceed with what they think is right, hopefully consistent with the consensus definition of "right direction." Most importantly, one-on-one, do something to help irrespective of consensus or lack thereof. My approach has been guided my beliefs rather than following the conventional wisdom.

What are you (the advice giver) doing now or going forward to help us move in the right direction? Not much. The paralysis of division is hamstringing consensus, resulting in the power struggle that is played out every day. The left and right, conservatives and liberals, democrats and republicans, whites and non-whites, male and female, citizens and non-citizens have their objectives regarding the right direction and they are aggressively and assertively exerting maximum influence to advance their objectives. We as 'normal folk,' preoccupied with the challenges of day-to-day survival, may think we are contributing by joining 'the movement' when all that is occurring is our pawnship in the chess game orchestrated by those in power. It is my strong belief that unity is sacrificed at the altar of divisiveness to increase the general dependence on government preferred by the left in pursuit of greater government which assures their incumbency. Unity thrives on lesser government which reduces the bureaucracy, thereby placing career politicians at risk. Recognizing that this is a controversial statement, I offer it with the following proposal as a first step toward my vision of the right direction: (1) As there is a constitutional limit on presidential terms, so too should there be limits on House and Senate terms; (2) reduce government salaries across the board, starting with Senate and House salaries at $100K with the same private sector health plans offered to the general population; those who say we must compete with the private sector to attract good talent have overplayed their hand. (3) eliminate pensions for all who work in the government sector, assuring that their service is one intended for public service and benefit rather than their own incumbencies; (4) in the tax code, eliminate the deductibility of any individual compensation: salary, stock, warrants, options, bonuses, etc. to $5 million; anything above that is not a deductible write-off against taxes (5) eliminate the deductibility of media advertising for pharmaceuticals (when was the last time you went to your doctor and asked her/him for the medicine you saw in a commercial?); (6) whenever a corporation eliminates domestic jobs and relocates them outside the US, the deductibility against taxes of the salaries, benefits and others costs related thereto are prohibited and whenever a corporation relocates jobs from offshore to the

US, they receive a tax credit for that year. (7) Create a citizen oversight committee to audit government expenditures, including the inexcusable excursions overseas as fact-finding missions.

What recommendation do you have to the advice seeker about how to help us collectively move in the right direction? Start with the definition of what the right direction is, being open to all considerations regardless of complexity or politicality. Establish a project timeline of five years by which to arrive at a consensus position paper, during which time the general population is encouraged to contribute their ideas online (with appropriate cybersecurity measures to eliminate bots, foreign entities, contribution by the political parties, etc., similar to that which the Census Bureau has deployed for the 2020 Census). As we vote our individual consciences during elections, we should be able to individually contribute to this effort to coalesce and move in the right direction.

(Ralph)

--

Paul, regarding giving advice, here are my brief thoughts:

1. Never give advice unless specifically asked. Even when you do, give all the caveats...just a point of view, one should do what they feel is right for them, etc.

2. Advice to your own family members, especially grown children, is to let them make their own choices, learn from their own mistakes, and give unsolicited advice only if they do or about to do something egregious...and that too only once.

3. As far as smaller children, especially teen agers is to give both sided of a recommendation and encourage them to do what they think is best.

This about sums it up!

(Sam)

———

Paul, here's my attempt to provide advice to someone who asks me how to live a good life:

What do we (collectively) need to do to move in the right direction? I would like to present "how to live the good life" in the following way. There are many opinions on how to conduct one's life. The road map for conducting a good life was laid around 340 BC by Aristotle in what some have called the best self-help book ever written. I refer to the ten books of the Nicomachean Ethics (Ethical Nicomachea.)

The books are an examination of the nature of the good life for a human being. The work begins with Aristotle positing that there exists some ultimate good toward which, in the final analysis, all human actions ultimately aim. The basic purpose of Ethics for Aristotle is the journey to become good. Achieving "goodness" depends upon developing character. The word character comes to us from a Greek word meaning etch or engrave. Accordingly, character is something that is enduring and stable.

Book 1 begins with the claim that "every art and every inquiry, and similarly every action and pursuit, is thought to aim at some good; and for this reason, the good has rightly been declared to be that at which all things aim." Something is "good" if it functions according to the purpose for which it was made.

Ethics is the best way to live the good life as you develop a virtuous character. The ultimate purpose of life is to achieve happiness. Wealth, honor, health, pleasure are the aspects of happiness that most human beings strive to achieve. A thorough analysis of these goals will lead us to realize that while they are necessary to some degree to survive, they will not lead to ultimate happiness if we pursue them to the nth degree. There are many wealthy people who are not happy. Wealth can bring power. It was said famously that absolute power corrupts absolutely. Aristotle says that power shows the person for what they are. Give someone a lot of resources and you will find out who they really are.

A total pursuit of pleasure would be akin to choosing the life of a fatted cattle. Many people seek honor. The best of us seek honor from the virtuous, they don't seek honor for its own sake. The danger here is that some might seek honor more than the qualities from which it arises.

All the above are components of the good life. The danger is pursuing them full bore to an unfulfilling life. The lesson of The Ethics is that our purpose on earth is to live the virtuous life. If we are faithful in that regard, all good things will come to us. Humans are empowered to make choices. Our souls have discretion over what we do and how we act. We can make who we ultimately are. There is something in our soul that is persuaded by reason. Aristotle was not a Christian but these thoughts echo Matthew 6:33: *"Seek ye therefore first the kingdom of God, and his justice, and all these things shall be added unto you."*

Finally, Aristotle connects his philosophy to Politics. (There is a separate work on Politics.) It is beyond my scope to discuss that lengthy work. The key point is that man is a political animal. We live in a hierarchy of family, village and community. Among all of creation, man is distinguished by the ability to speak. Speech allows us to express our opinions about what is good, bad, just and unjust. Therefore, man alone has the ability to perceive good and bad. Community in these things is what makes a city.

What role does empathy have in the direction we should take? I have said Aristotle described the traits that are unique to human beings. While creativity and community are important as mentioned above, empathy is at the top of the list of uniquely human traits. Humans have to ability to sympathize and perceive the feelings of another." Aristotle says that happiness derives from developing our uniquely human traits, not so much our rationality, but a focus on empathy. Empathy is at the core of how we understand our fellow human beings; it is what it means to be human. I already mention the echo I see in the Gospel of that the first commandment is loving God above all things, And the second is like unto it, Matthew 22-39-40…"*Thou shalt love thy neighbor as thyself. On these two commandments hang all the law and the prophets.*"

But empathy is not merely the expression of emotion. Many today exalt emotion without its necessary companion of knowledge. I think it would be instructive if some of us guidance from what we call The Great Books (reference is https://en.wikipedia.org/wiki/Great_books). Charles Dickens is included in later editions of the Great Books. Dickens was an outspoken social critic in general, but especially about poverty. But a scene Dicken's "A Christmas Carol" has always resonated with me when thinking about how to administer social justice. "*This boy is Ignorance. This girl is Want. Beware them both, and all of their degree, but most of all beware this boy, for on his brow I see that written which is Doom, unless the writing be erased.*"

While showing Scrooge the pitiful children, he is telling all of humankind that they represent Man's mortal enemies -- the condition of Want (for food, shelter, etc.) where millions endure and live through daily. But most especially living in a self-imposed Ignorance; the Ignorance in which Man chooses to live his life. Human beings, according the Spirit, must wake up and see what is needed by others and the role each individual can play to assuage the pain and suffering of his brothers and sisters in this world. The warning is that, unless we wake from a self-imposed Ignorance, we he will bring about our own downfall, our collective "Doom."

What are you (the Advice giver) doing now or going forward to help us move in the right direction? Since we posit that the best kind of life is one where we are happy to be fully human and to conduct ourselves in an ethical and virtuous manner, ensure that you live in a civil society where you can be free.

What recommendation do you have to the advice seeker about how to help us collectively move in the right direction? Taken from the last paragraph in the Nicomachean Ethics - Book X. Ch. 9, I would say that the best way for us to thrive as individuals, family, village and community (city) is by taking the advice offered to us by Aristotle in the discussion below.

"But it is difficult to hit upon a right training toward virtue from youth when one has not been brought up under the laws of that sort, for living temperately and with endurance is not pleasant to most people, especially not to the young. Hence it is necessary to arrange for rearing and exercises by laws, since they will not be painful when they have become habitual.

First then, if anything partial has been well said by our predecessors, let us try to go through it, and then on the basis of the collection of constitutions to look at what sorts of things preserve and destroy cities and what sorts do so for each sort of constitution and for what reasons some are governed well and others are the reverse. For when these things have been examined perhaps we might also have more insight into what sort of constitution is best and how each sort is to be arranged and by using what laws and customs. So, having made a beginning, let us discuss it."

Aristotle closes the Book as he points to the constitution. It would be well for us all to remember that.

(Mike M.)

--

Hi Paul,

I enjoyed the podcast! And I truly agree with the content. I have always figured that I learn as much from teaching as the students do. I would say in fact that there is no better way to learn material than to teach! I also wondered whether this argument might have relevance for the crime problems in Baltimore. We sponsored a research project recently where the investigators hung out in a predominantly African American barber shop. They found that this was a great environment to get some honest opinions from everyday people. One of the striking things they found is that a huge number of the people coming through this barber shop had criminal records--and not just for once but often many times - lie a revolving door. Another fascinating finding is that these repeat offenders were very concerned about what was going to happen to children in their communities. It sounds counter intuitive at first, but I wonder what would happen if you matched guys getting out of prison with juveniles at risk from the same neighborhoods in some sort of teaching environment?

(Gary)

———

I think we are limited in using words to give advice to others. I know myself that when I have asked others for advice, it's oftentimes for the purpose getting affirmation for what I am planning to do anyway. I think that actions are a much more powerful way to set an example.

I love to engage in discussions about "meaning", "purpose of life", etc. I've found that asking other people questions about what they think AND actually listening to their responses is much more productive than asking and then waiting for the entree point to interrupt and provide my opinions. After doing this (asking for the purpose telling), I've learned the other person's response is much more meaningful than my (to me) tired recitation of my beliefs.

But...., since you asked, here's what I would say:

At some point in my life, I started experiencing persistent anxiety, insomnia, and generalized body pain. I felt that my religious background, which focused on an afterlife for people who followed the "rules", did not provide useful guidance. In the very few times I was able to quiet myself I felt like I heard a message that I was supposed to help others. So I did. I felt a significant amount of inertia getting started, but I found structured one-on-one volunteering. After getting in to this, I started to find reasons why this was the wrong solution - flaws in the volunteer program or concept, flaws in my volunteering capabilities, and general lethargy (what's the point anyway?). But somehow I have stuck with it and it is one of the best things I have done.

I still have persistent anxiety, insomnia, and generalized body pain, but I did develop a viewpoint that makes all of those things tolerable.

The viewpoint is that there is no substance or meaning to ourselves alone. The only meaning we have is as part of a singular organism of all living things. We have egos because they are needed to achieve the purposes of evolution but the belief in an individual ego or soul is an illusion that makes many of us selfish and that makes us unhappy.

Realizing this doesn't really change anything - realizing this and spending the rest of my life living this through actions can, I think.

So, to summarize, I think that would be my advice to someone - one day you may be confronted a realization that focusing your ego or following someone else's code for life becomes unsatisfying. And you might find that society's solutions - medications, distractions, religions, etc. do not help. If you're like me, my only suggestion is that you'll have to figure it out yourself. Don't get logged into "isms" and don't get frustrated. To me, at least at this point, my purpose is two-fold - to find meaning and to help others. Find out what your purpose is - don't let me tell you what it is.

Fun project! What's next?

AFTERWORD

So that's what we came up with. Did we come up with a magic
bullet to make us truly aware of each other and to consider the impact of our actions on each other before we act? No, we simply
don't have and can't have this ability – and if we did, I believe we
would be unable to take any action at all.

I think we learned that, to come up with a "wider" understanding,
we need to confront some unpleasant aspects of ourselves. I use
the term "wider" in the context of Albert Einstein's quote:

> *"A human being is a part of the whole called by us universe, a part
> limited in time and space. He experiences himself, his thoughts and
> feeling as something separated from the rest, a kind of optical delu-
> sion of his consciousness. This delusion is a kind of prison for us, re-
> stricting us to our personal desires and to affection for a few persons
> nearest to us. Our task must be to free ourselves from this prison by
> widening our circle of compassion to embrace all living creatures and
> the whole of nature in its beauty."*

There are multiple and different definitions of empathy and compassion. I have come to look at empathy as the emotion, which, if
intentionally developed, and balanced by with analytical thought,

can help us achieve the two things that I think should be our two lifelong objectives – wisdom and compassion.

One last thought – one of this project's collaborators and one of the people I most look to for wisdom and perspective shared this quote with me recently from Bishop Desmond Tutu:

> *"It is awesome that God the Omnipotent One depends on us fragile and vulnerable creatures to accomplish God's will and to bring justice and healing and wholeness. God has no one but us."*

I love that idea. Let's keep trying to bringing justice and healing and wholeness.

Want to participate in the next one? Send me an email to: *what.have.you.learned.so.far.com*

11/28/2019 Thanksgiving Day